THE ILLUSTRATED ENCYCLOPEDIA OF

VOLUME 5

The Mammals

Part V

Wildlife Consultant

MARY CORLISS PEARL, Ph. D.

Distributed by Encyclopaedia Britannica
Educational Corporation

Grey Castle Press

Published by Grey Castle Press, 1991

Distributed by Encyclopaedia Britannica Educational Corporation, 1991

THE ILLUSTRATED ENCYCLOPEDIA OF WILDLIFE
Volume 5: THE MAMMALS—Part V

Library of Congress Cataloging-in-Publication Data
The Illustrated encyclopedia of wildlife.
    p.   cm.
    Contents: v. 1–5. The mammals—v. 6–8. The birds —
v. 9. Reptiles and amphibians — v. 10. The fishes —
v. 11–14. The invertebrates — v. 15. The invertebrates
and index.
    ISBN 1–55905–052–7
    1. Zoology.
QL45.2.I44 1991   90–3750
591—dc20   CIP

ISBN 1–55905–052–7 (complete set)
    1–55905–041–1 (Volume 5)

Printed in Spain

Photo Credits
Photographs were supplied by *Ardea*: 800; *Archivio IGDA*: (S. Spini) 900; *Art Directors*: (B. Rybolt) 898; *Bruce Coleman*: 754, 810, 811, 814, 830, 846, 857, 889; (H. Albrecht) 717, 727, 868l, 870, 871, 873, 874, 875, 878, 879, 883t, 884, 885, 887; (J. & D. Bartlett) 746, 747, 749, 802, 825, 867t; (S.C. Bisserot) 804t, 821, 872t; (M. Boulton) 801l; (W. Boyer) 853; (J. Burton) 750, 757b, 832, 833; (R.I.M. Campbell) 755; (G. Cubitt) 737, 791; (P. Davey) 805b, 877; (L.R. Dawson) 823; (J. Ehbers) 718b; (M.P.L. Fogden) 753; (M. Freeman) 779, 801r, 829b; (C.B. Frith) 730t; (F. Futil) 845t; (D. Goulston) 807b; (C. Hughes) 734; (M. Kawai) 797; (L. Lyon) 858, 862, 864, 865t; (N. Myers) 733l, 738l; (G.D. Plage) 808, 831, 865b, 869; (M.P. Price) 719, 854l, 854r; (H. Reinhard) 760b, 805t; (F. Sauer) 752r; (Sullivan & Rogers) 775, 776, 777; (K. Taylor) 872b; (N. Tomalin) 739, 764, 769, 794, 813, 815l, 820t, 844, 845b; (S. Trevor) 817; (R. Williams) 718t, 720r, 729, 730b, 735l, 735r, 736l, 780, 784, 796, 815r, 819, 826, 834, 840, 883b; (J. Van Wormer) 770; (G. Ziesler) 765t; 772b, 773; (C. Zuber) 724, 725, 741b, 742, 743, 745, 772t, 882l; *Jacana*: (A. Bertrand) 722, 731, 848, 849l, 867b; (F. Boizot) 886; (J. Brun) 807t; (Champroux) 834, 835; (CNRS-Devez) 751t, 820b, 849r, 866, 881; (Frevet) 752l; (Frederic) 804b; (Hladik) 721, 782; (J.M. Labat) 726; (F. Petter) 822; (A. Rainon) 829t; (J. Ronert) 723; (J.X. Sundance) 863; (R. Tercafs) 748; (J.P. Varin) 736b, 740, 741t, 757r, 759, 760t, 763, 765b, 781, 787t, 803, 812, 828, 837, 838, 839, 841, 842, 843, 850, 851, 856, 859, 861b, 868r, 880, 882r, 888; (Varin-Visage) 728, 730, 733r, 738r, 756l, 758r, 761, 768, 771tr, 778, 785l, 785r, 786, 787b, 788, 789, 790, 793, 809, 827t, 827b, 855, 860, 861t; (Vasselet) 751b; (R. Volot) 774; (Ziesler) 756r, 766, 767, 771tl, 771b; *J. Nance-Magnum*: 892, 893; *Orion Press/NHPA*: 798, 799; *Tim Woodcock*: (Jennie Woodcock) 894; *Tony Stone Associates*: 891.

FRONT COVER: Western lowland gorilla with young (Ardea/K.W. Fink)

CONTENTS

LIFE IN THE TREES

From the lemurs of Madagascar to gorillas and human beings, the primates show a common dexterity, sharp vision and brain power that increase up the evolutionary ladder

Some people may think that they belong to an order of their own, separate from animals and their ancestry, but in fact they do not. Humans are biologically members of the primate order that also includes apes, monkeys, tarsiers, bush babies, lorises, and lemurs.

Most anthropologists believe that primitive primates living in North America and Eurasia, about 70 million years ago, may have been the earliest ancestors of today's primates (including humans). These first primates were small insect eaters that scurried about in the undergrowth and took to living in the trees about 60 million years ago. From North America and Eurasia they moved down into South America and Africa (at that time the continents were still one landmass), and evolved separately in these two areas. It is also generally recognized that Africa saw the rise of the more recent ancestors of human beings.

A tree shrew enigma

Until recently, some scientists argued that the tree shrews of Southeast Asia were the forerunners of primates, and classified them within the primate order. But it was never clear whether tree shrews were a branch of the insectivores or the primates, or whether they and the other two groups arose from a shared primitive ancestor. Today, tree shrews are classified neither with insectivores nor with primates but in an order of their own. They form a vital link in the evolutionary chain of both insectivores and primates, but it is still a mystery as to where in the chain the link belongs.

TOP LEFT The common tree shrew has certain characteristics that resemble those of primates. It has large eyes encircled by bone, possesses a well-developed brain and spends much of its life in the branches of trees. However, most zoologists now place the 18 species of tree shrews in a separate order from the primates — the apparent similarities between the two groups are thought to have probably evolved quite independently.

LEFT The macaque monkeys live in a wide variety of habitats from the high mountains of Tibet to the tropical rain forests of Indonesia. Some species, such as rhesus and bonnet macaques, have adapted to urban environments and have become pests in some of India's largest cities.
PAGE 717 The chimpanzee is one of the most highly developed of the primates, with many features, both physical and behavioral, that are strikingly similar to those of humans.

RIGHT **A young orangutan uses its long arms and its legs to clamber about among the branches of rain forest trees. Its thumb opposes (or faces) the fingers, enabling it to grip tightly to the branches.**
BELOW RIGHT **Hands compared: the common tree shrew (A); the aye-aye,** a prosimian (B); the gibbon, an ape that swings from branches (C); the chimpanzee, a great ape (D); and the human being (E). The development of hands that are able to grasp and manipulate objects comes to a peak in the great apes and in humans.

Most people think of chimpanzees, gorillas and gibbons when they think of primates. But the primate order also includes lemurs, lorises and bush babies, tarsiers and capuchin monkeys, marmosets and tamarins, aggressive baboons and macaques, and the peaceful vegetarian giants of tropical forests, like the gorilla and orang-utan. They live almost entirely in the warmer parts of the world, but have adapted to a wide range of habitats. Some are nocturnal, others are mainly active in the day; some live mainly on the ground, others in trees. Many species live in tropical rain forests, but some have adapted to life in dry, rocky areas. There are specialized fruit eaters as well as specialized leaf eaters.

During early primate history, tarsiers, bush babies, and lorises dominated the forests and spread throughout much of Africa and Asia. Lemurs evolved in isolation on the island of Madagascar, off the south-eastern coast of Africa. They have had no competition from other primates for the last 50 million years, because the island is known to have been separated from mainland Africa for at least that long. Lemurs have also been free from the many predators that hunt primates in Africa—leopards, for example, which are major predators of baboons. Fossil records show that lemurs evolved into well over 40 distinct species in Madagascar, but now only 20 species remain.

An early modification

One of the first and most important events to take place during primate evolution was a change in the shape of the hands and feet, so that primates could grip the branches while climbing trees. Rodents and tree shrews climb trees by digging their claws (fingernails) into the bark. With these animals, each finger and toe ends in a strong claw fused to the end of the last bone of the finger or toe. The fleshy pad on the base of the hands and feet is merely a fixed cushion of

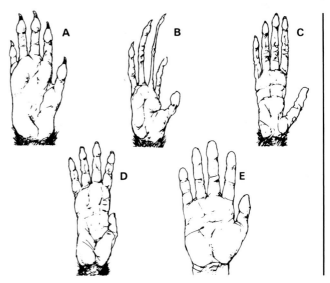

ABOVE Verraux's sifaka is a member of the lemur family. It is most active during the day, and can make huge leaps between trees using its powerful legs; its short arms are comparatively under-developed.
ABOVE RIGHT Gibbons' eyes face forward, enabling them to judge accurately the distances between branches and to identify rapidly all possible foot-holds and handholds. In contrast to the sifaka, they rely on their arms when moving through the trees, swinging from one branch to another with astonishing speed and agility.

hard skin to provide support for the claw and to absorb impact—it is not there to provide grip.

The evolution of primates took a different direction to that of the rodents. Claws became gradually flatter and narrower as fingers lengthened and the end bones became flatter. The fleshy hand and foot pads became less thick and grew underneath each finger and toe. These changes resulted in pads that are sensitive to touch. The most important reasons for the evolution of flat nails was that while long claws are good for climbing up trees and along branches (as in squirrels), they are not good for hanging from branches, for swinging from one branch to the next (called brachiating), or for reaching out and picking off leaves or fruit from the trees. Primates use both their hands and their feet for these purposes.

The revolutionary thumb

As the primates evolved, so their fingers and toes became more flexible. Eventually, the thumb developed so that it could be rotated and pressed against any one of the fingers. This gave the animal a good grip and, more importantly, precision in manipulating things. For example, with an opposable thumb (it can face, or oppose, the other fingers) the human hand can pick up tiny objects without breaking or dropping them. A chimpanzee can hold a small twig between thumb and forefinger, using it as a tool to extract termites from their mounds.

The shape of primate hands depends on the animals' way of life. The macaques have short thumbs because they are basically ground-dwelling animals and walk with their palms flat on the ground; gibbons have opposable thumbs, but these are well spaced from their fingers, which are used for hanging from branches. Tamarins, however, have claws instead of flattened fingernails—an unusual characteristic among the monkeys and apes. These adaptations of the hands and feet allow the monkeys to feed with ease in the forest trees. They can hold onto the larger branches with both hands and both feet and pull tiny branches toward them, picking off the leaves or fruit that they want.

LIFE IN THE TREES

Improved eyesight

Primitive primates had to be able to judge distances accurately as they leaped from branch to branch and tree to tree. In order to do this, the eyes gradually moved, during the course of evolution, from the side of the head to the front. The more they faced forward, the more each eye's field of vision overlapped, giving the animal a wider "binocular vision." Tree shrews, animals low down the evolutionary ladder, have only minimal binocular vision. Their eyes are at the side of their head, and although they see well to the side and rear, the area where the vision of each eye overlaps is small. The advanced primates, such as gorillas, have eyes at the front of their head, and have a far wider overlap, giving them wide binocular vision. The eyes of all primates are enclosed in bony sockets, called orbits, that support and protect them.

As they evolved, many primates became less nocturnal and developed color vision, increasing their efficiency at finding food and mates, and avoiding predators. Primates that remained nocturnal, such as the tarsiers and bush babies, have larger eyes than those of animals that are active during the day, enabling them to see in the dark.

A reduced sense of smell

As eyesight became more effective through the course of primate evolution, smell became less important. Behavior based on an ability to smell, such as marking territory with urine, feces or glandular secretions, started to disappear. The changes to eyes, feet and smell are more pronounced as one moves from the prosimians, or "lower primates",

BELOW A group of female langur monkeys tend their own young, and will also baby-sit for the infants of other females. From lemurs and bush babies through to chimpanzees and humans, there is a marked increase in the amount of time young primates spend with their parents. During the period of parental care, the young will learn all they need for survival once they become independent.

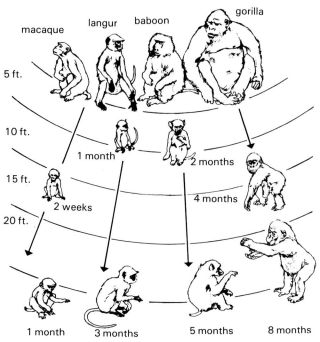

ABOVE Among chimpanzees, the period of parental care of offspring is longer than for all other primates apart from humans. Young chimps remain with their mothers until they are at least five years old.

ABOVE RIGHT Monkeys and apes keep a close watch on the movements of their young offspring. The diagram indicates the distances that parents of the different species allow their young to roam. In each case the distances increase as the young grow older, but the rate at which they increase varies greatly from one species to another. After only a month a young macaque may be allowed to stray as far as 20 ft. from its mother. A young gorilla has to wait until it is eight months old before it enjoys the same freedom.

(lemurs, lorises, pottos, bush babies and tarsiers) to the "higher primates," the monkeys and apes.

In adapting to life in the trees, primates underwent a variety of changes to the shapes of their bodies, and to their diet and reproduction. The period of gestation became longer, and the pregnant female's placenta (the spongy organ in the uterus that nourishes the unborn offspring, or fetus) gradually developed, increasing the supply of blood and nutrients from the mother to the fetus. Having given birth, the length of time devoted by the mother to looking after, protecting and training the young one also increased.

Care of the infant

The growing amount of parental care given by primates to their offspring played an important part in primate evolution. Females stopped producing large litters, since the demands on the mothers would have been too great. Instead, the majority of primates began to have one offspring at a time. In the higher primates, parental care becomes more complex. Education is part of an extended parental care period in humans, necessary both for the survival of the offspring and for the success of the species.

One of the most distinctive differences between apes and monkeys can be seen in the way they move around. Monkeys and apes are basically quadrupedal—they move about on all fours. Some monkeys, however, have prehensile (grasping) tails that serve as a fifth limb for hanging from branches. Others, such as spider monkeys, have especially long arms for swinging along branches (a method of locomotion known as brachiation).

In contrast to monkeys, apes do not have tails, and the gibbons (or lesser apes) are the only apes to have developed brachiation to any great degree. Gibbons regularly walk on their hind legs only, in an upright position known as bipedal walking—just as humans do. Gorillas and chimpanzees are also capable of

walking on their hind legs, and do so quite often. The great apes (gorilla, chimpanzee and orangutan) do not swing from branches like gibbons. The current opinion among zoologists is that man's closest relatives are the great apes.

The primate features

To understand the order that represents the peak of mammalian evolution, it is useful to look at some of the general features of the primates as a whole. Prosimians are often described as the "lower primates" because they are lower down the evolutionary ladder. They have smaller brains than monkeys and apes and a far more highly developed sense of smell. They have longer snouts, and many species have dog-like faces.

Monkeys and apes, the "higher primates," live more by their wits. They have larger brains than the lower

ABOVE **Young baboons are allowed to ride on their mothers' backs until they are about seven months old. Males within a troop of baboons will help in transporting the young, and since they are much larger than females, they provide** extra protection from predators such as lions and cheetahs.

PAGES 724-725 Ring-tailed lemurs are gregarious animals, foraging in mixed groups that may contain 30 or more females, males and their young.

primates, a more highly developed sense of sight than smell, and they have tended to evolve flatter faces (although the drills and baboons have particularly long muzzles). Instead of having large olfactory lobes in the brain for the sense of smell (as the prosimians have), higher primates have a more developed cerebral cortex—the area of the brain concerned with skilled movements, vision, intelligence and speech.

LEFT AND ABOVE Gibbons are the most adept of the brachiating primates — animals that move about by swinging from branch to branch. Their arms are longer than their legs and their thumbs are short so that they do not obstruct the animals' swinging action. The gibbons' fast passage through the trees enables them to reach food sources and escape from dangerous predators very quickly.

Clues in the teeth

The fossil records of primates are far from complete. Much of what is known is based on the structure of their teeth, since the teeth are the longest-lasting parts of the skeleton. All primates have four types of teeth: incisors for cutting, canines for piercing and tearing, and premolars and molars for crushing and grinding. The ancestors of primates ate insects, and had teeth adapted for that purpose. As the primate diet gradually changed from insects to leaves and fruit, some of the many sharp, pointed teeth gave way to fewer but much larger, flatter teeth that were ideal for grinding. Leaf-eating monkeys have ridges across their premolar teeth for grinding fibrous fruit and vegetation.

As humans and their ancestors developed weapons for defense, they lost the need for large canine teeth to threaten and bite intruders found on their territory. Canine teeth have become insignificant in humans, but they are still strongly evident in other primates and are often used in threat displays.

ABOVE **Chimpanzees normally walk on all fours, though they sometimes stand erect and may walk a few paces on just two feet. When moving on all fours, they place the knuckles of their hands on the ground rather than resting on their** palms like monkeys. RIGHT **The family tree of the present-day primates shows how the different groups have evolved from common ancestors and diversified over the last 50 million years.**

As primates evolved and needed to deal with more and more information, their brain size increased. A human brain averages around 84 cu. in., while that of the smaller prosimians is only about 0.1 cu. in. To accommodate such changes, the skull grew larger, but its basic structure stayed the same.

Swinging and walking

The first true primates probably walked on all fours (they were quadrupedal), and had long tails, long backs, and narrow ribcages. Lemurs and, to a lesser extent, baboons, still retain this basic shape. But the shapes of other primate species have changed according to their means of getting about or in reaction to their environment. Tarsiers developed long hind legs for leaping from one tree trunk to another, while gibbons, which swing along in the branches,

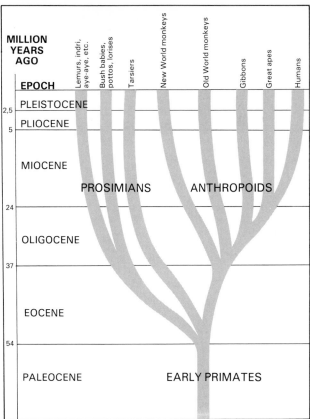

The order Primates contains over 180 species, grouped into two distinct suborders. The suborder Prosimii—the prosimians or lower primates—includes the lemurs, the dwarf lemurs, the mouse lemurs, the indri, the sifakas, the aye-aye, the bush babies, the potto, the lorises, and the tarsiers. They comprise six families in all.

Monkeys and apes belong to the suborder Anthropoidae—the anthropoids or higher primates. Also containing six families, the suborder comprises the New World monkeys (including marmosets, tamarins, capuchins, howlers, and spider monkeys); the Old World monkeys (including macaques, baboons, mangabeys, guenons, langurs, and leaf monkeys); the apes (the gibbons, the orangutan, the gorilla, and the chimpanzees); and the hominids (today represented only by the human being).

LEFT In terms of physical and behavioral evolution, the gorilla is one of the closest primates to humans. Despite its fearsome appearance, it is a peaceful vegetarian. Unfortunately, the numbers of gorillas are dwindling, mainly due to destruction of their forest habitat.
RIGHT A teething, long-haired spider monkey, just three months old, chews on a forest leaf.

have much longer arms than legs. Some species favored an upright stance so that they could keep a lookout for danger on the ground and be able to reach further for food. These primates developed shorter, more robust backbones and pelvises, and larger chests. Humans' arms are shorter than their legs, which evolved for fast running.

The shape of hands and feet reflect the way that primates move. Monkeys that walk on all fours have short thumbs and big toes, and long, narrow feet. Gibbons have long fingers with which to swing through the trees. Their thumbs are comparatively short, since their hands hook onto the branches with their fingers, rather than grasping them with fingers and thumb. Apes, such as gorillas and orangutans, have highly developed, opposable thumbs and big toes for gripping branches. Humans have the same shaped hands as apes, but their feet are quite different—the toe bones are greatly reduced in length and the big toe is not opposable.

Human origins

There has been endless controversy over the origin of humans, with little agreement among zoologists as to which of the present-day great apes is closest to man. The answer depends a great deal on which criteria are used and which pieces of evidence are included or ignored. The similarities between any one great ape and human ancestors may be more a reflection of adaptation to similar life-styles and diet, rather than of a direct evolutionary relationship. However, most scientists agree that by 20 million years ago the ancestors of humans had become quite separate from all the other primates (see pages 891-900).

TOP Common tree shrews often rub their bodies against branches, leaving trails of scent from glands on their chests. Though good climbers, they spend much of the time on the forest floor, foraging in leaf litter for insects, worms, seeds and fruit.

ABOVE The bushy tails of Indian tree shrews give the animals a superficial resemblance to squirrels, and their semi-terrestrial habits are also similar. Indeed, the tree shrews' alternative name, the tupaia, is the Malay word for squirrel.

TREE SHREWS

An order apart

Formerly grouped with the primates, but now considered by most zoologists to represent an order of their own (the Scandentia), the tree shrews are rain forest inhabitants of India, Southeast Asia, Indonesia and the Philippines. They are small mammals, measuring some 8-16 in. including their long tails. They have shrew-like snouts and claws on all their digits. Some species spend most of their lives in the branches of trees, while other species spend much of the time foraging on the ground. They eat a variety of plant and animal foods, and some of the larger species may catch creatures the size of small lizards and rodents.

The common tree shrew is the species that has been most studied in the wild. It is a territorial animal, scent-marking and defending home ranges that cover about 2.5 acres of forested land. Each home range is normally occupied by an adult pair and their young, but although the tree shrews share the same space, the family group is a fairly loose association and the animals tend to forage separately.

Most of the tree shrews make their nests in hollow trees. From one to three young are born, and while they remain in the nest they receive only infrequent visits from their mother. She returns to suckle them every few days, and between suckling periods they are left completely alone. Such a limited amount of parental care is unusual among mammals and stands in marked contrast to the intensive care that most of the primates provide for their offspring.

The 18 species of tree shrews are all members of the family Tupaiidae, and all but one are grouped into the subfamily Tupaiinae. They include the common tree shrew, *Tupaia glis*, of Sumatra and the Malay Peninsula; the Indian tree shrew, *Anathana ellioti*, of India; and the terrestrial tree shrew, *Lyonogale tana*, that lives mainly on the forest floor in Borneo and Sumatra. The pen-tailed tree shrew, *Ptilocercus lowii*, of Malaysia, Borneo, and Sumatra is the sole member of the subfamily Ptilocercinae. Unlike the other tree shrews, it is nocturnal and rarely descends to ground level.

EYES TO
THE FORE

Occupying a rung in primate evolution below monkeys and apes, the prosimians share one striking feature—large, forward-facing eyes

Greater weasel lemur

Fork-crowned
dwarf lemur

Verreaux's sifaka

Ring-tailed
lemur

Brown lesser
mouse lemur

Black lemur (male)

Aye-aye

The prosimians are a varied group of 35 species divided into six main families: lemurs; dwarf lemurs and mouse lemurs; indris and sifakas; aye-ayes; bush babies, pottos and lorises; and tarsiers.

Although lemurs are confined to the island of Madagascar off the southeast coast of Africa, the prosimians as a whole are distributed across Africa and much of Southeast Asia. They are mainly forest dwellers, eating fruit or leaves, although the ring-tailed lemur is omnivorous (feeding on many kinds of food, including flesh).

The sizes of the prosimians range from about 5 in. in the lesser mouse lemurs, which are the smallest of all primates, to as much as 35 in. long in the indri. The hands and feet of prosimians are similar to monkeys, with broad pads and flat fingernails and toenails. Like the higher primates, prosimians have opposable thumbs for gripping branches. Some prosimians live almost entirely in trees, while others find their food on the ground. Most species have long, soft fur and are nocturnal. Those that are active during the day include the ring-tailed lemur, the indri and two of the three species of sifakas.

Night eyes

The eyes of nocturnal prosimians, such as tarsiers, are huge and superbly adapted to seeing in the dark. The retina of each eye (the area at the back of the eyeball onto which light falls) has a high concentration of light-receptive cells. These enable the animal to pick up the slightest changes in the intensity of the light. The tarsier's eyes are so acute that the animal can

BELOW LEFT The lemurs are confined to Madagascar and nearby islands in the Indian Ocean, and most are restricted to small areas within even this limited range. Black lemurs live only in the western part of north Madagascar.
BELOW Even with her single offspring clinging to her back, a female Verreaux's sifaka can climb trees with great ease.
PAGE 731 The huge eyes of the slender loris are adapted for night vision, allowing the animal to judge shapes and distances accurately after dark in the forests of India and Sri Lanka.

accurately judge leaps between trees in the middle of the night. An indication of the importance of eyes to tarsiers is their sheer size relative to the size of the body. In the western tarsier, each eye is 0.6 in. across and weighs more than the animal's brain.

The prosimians' eyes are enclosed in bony sockets, or orbits, in the skull and are positioned in the front of the face for binocular vision. A raised strip of bone running around the outer edge of the eye socket protects and supports the outer section of the eyes. The tarsier's eyes, like those of owls, can hardly move within their bony armor. The lemurs of Madagascar have become less nocturnal and more active during the day, possibly because there are no dangerous predators to contend with (apart from humans), as there are for the mainland primates. It also reflects a growing trend toward daytime activity in the primate family as a whole.

The supremacy of smell

Prosimians retain many of the characteristics of primitive apes and monkeys. The most important of these is a highly developed sense of smell, which has been lost among higher primates. Many of the prosimians, therefore, have long snouts like other animals that rely on smell for finding food. But their

ABOVE Bush babies have a much wider distribution than the lemurs, occurring over much of mainland Africa in forests, wooded savannas, and even mango and coffee plantations and suburban gardens. Like the lorises, they are nocturnal animals and are adapted for catching their prey in the dark. When they see an insect, small reptile or small bird, they leap on it with a lightning pounce, killing it with a bite and chewing it up. They usually sit on their haunches when eating.

sense of smell is not, as with most other mammals, solely for finding food. Smell is also an important part of communication. Prosimians possess scent glands, which they use to mark certain branches. Scent communication is almost absent in higher primates— but not totally. Humans use scent (perfume) to attract a partner, and substances known as pheromones are important in sexual attraction in humans (they can be found in, for example, fresh sweat).

The teeth of prosimians are more like those of their insectivore ancestors than those of higher primates. Most lemurs, lorises and bush babies have small upper incisors, while the incisors and canines in the lower jaw lie almost flat, forming a type of grooming comb. The aye-aye is unique among primates in that it has large, powerful incisors that never stop growing (also a characteristic of rodents).

Lemurs of Madagascar

How lemurs came to be on the island of Madagascar is a mystery, but fossils prove that they have been there for at least 50 million years. They have evolved in isolation from other monkeys and apes, but have still developed many of the features possessed by primates living on the African mainland, South America and Asia.

Lemurs have no competition from other monkeys, nor do they have to contend with such mainland predators as leopards and jackals. On Madagascar's safe island environment more than 40 species of lemurs evolved. Some, now extinct, were the size of orangutans. When humans arrived on the island about 2000 years ago, many species of lemurs were quickly wiped out by hunting and competition from introduced domestic animals, such as cattle and goats. More than 20 lemur species remain, and these are divided into four families: true lemurs, dwarf lemurs and mouse lemurs; the aye-aye (just one species); and indris and sifakas.

Most lemurs have long, bushy tails that they use as a counterbalance when jumping. The indri, however, has a tail only two inches long, yet this does not seem to affect its amazing leaping ability. Lemurs also have long snouts, and their hind legs are far more

ABOVE LEFT **The fat-tailed dwarf lemur has a low body temperature and a poor system of heat regulation. It is therefore forced to hibernate in winter and survives by using up the reserves of fat that are stored in its long, thick tail.** ABOVE **The gray lesser** mouse lemur is one of the smallest of the primates, measuring less than 5 in. in length and weighing about 2 oz. Despite its tiny size, it feeds on prey as large as frogs and lizards, as well as on insects, fruit and the gum from trees.

developed than their forelegs, enabling them to leap several yards between branches and trees. They are very acrobatic, even on high, spindly branches. The ring-tailed lemur is the only lemur to spend much of its time on the ground—when it does climb trees, it stays on horizontal, usually wide branches.

Scented communication

The lemurs have scent glands with which they mark the branches of their territories. The striking bands on the tail of the ring-tailed lemur provide obvious visual signals. But these animals also smear glandular secretions over their tails and wave the scented warning signal at potential rivals. Some lemurs also communicate vocally, making loud calls to tell other members of a group where they are, and to warn animals from neighboring groups against coming

The prosimians range over Africa, Madagascar, India, Southeast Asia and Indonesia.

any closer. A mixture of vocal and olfactory (smell) signals ensure that different lemur groups keep a reasonable distance from one another. Calls may also serve as alarm signals when a source of danger has entered the forest.

Lemurs are vegetarians. Unlike higher primates, they never use their hands to pick their food, but merely pull branches toward their mouths and bite off what they want. Diet varies from species to species and, to a certain extent, from season to season. The animal known as a gentle lemur eats mainly the shoots and leaves of young bamboo. Unfortunately, bamboo

LEFT A ruffed lemur displays the long, dog-like snout typical of lemurs. Like most prosimians, lemurs have an acute sense of smell both for finding food and for communication—they frequently scent-mark their territories to warn neighboring groups of their presence.
BELOW Female red-fronted lemurs have striking facial markings and soft, reddish brown fur. They usually have one offspring, or occasionally twins—born fully furred and with their eyes open.

only grows in a small, wet part of the island and it is rapidly being cut down by the local people. The result is that gentle lemurs are losing their habitat and becoming increasingly rare.

During the dry season, the mongoose lemur eats mainly nectar from flowers. The Mayotte lemur eats fruit when in season; when fruit is not available it changes its diet to leaves. Some species that have a nutritionally poor diet eat their own feces in order to reabsorb nutrients that have been excreted.

The isolated lemurs

Lemurs live only on Madagascar and the nearby Comoro Islands, separated from mainland Africa by the Mozambique Channel. Until a few thousand years ago there was a great range of lemurs on Madagascar—some as small as a shrew and others as large as an orangutan. Some were active by day (diurnal), others were nocturnal. They lived both in trees and on the ground. Then humans arrived. The lemurs were hunted for food and driven from land as it was settled, and as the trees were felled for firewood, logging and the spread of agriculture.

Domestic animals competed with the native ones—as has happened so often when humans have colonized islands—and the lemurs suffered a catastrophic decline. Many species became extinct, so that the lemurs of today probably represent only about half of the species that existed a few thousand years ago. Many, if not all, of the present-day lemurs are threatened by the continuing loss of their habitats—the forests and bamboo groves of Madagascar.

Most lemurs have an adaptation that equips them for night vision. In common with other nocturnal mammals, such as cats, they have a layer of cells, known as the *tapetum lucidum*, behind the retinas of their eyes. Light entering the eye is reflected back to pass through the retina a second time, ensuring that the maximum amount of light in the dimness of the night is detected. It is the *tapetum* that is responsible for making the eyes shine like a cat's eyes when a torch or photographer's flashlight is aimed at the animal's

RIGHT A female black lemur keeps a sharp eye out for danger from her perch. To escape from predators, black lemurs flee through the trees, then suddenly drop to the ground and run quickly through the vegetation until they reach a safer tree, where they can take refuge.

ABOVE **Two female black lemurs flanking a young male show the extreme differences of color between the sexes. Whereas the males are uniformly black, the females are reddish brown** with white ear tufts and dark-brown faces. The two sexes were at one time even regarded as separate species.
ABOVE RIGHT **The nectar-eating mongoose lemur, like the closely related** brown lemur, can be found in Madagascar and the Comoro Islands off its northwest coast. Both species were probably taken to the smaller islands by the original settlers, and the lemurs are now threatened by loss of habitat.
BELOW **Both ring-tailed lemurs (A) and sifakas (B) are sun lovers and will sit on the branches, arms outstretched, soaking up the sun's heat.**

face. It is this feature, combined with their tendency to call loudly at night, that earned the lemurs their name—"lemur" meaning "ghost." In ancient Rome the "lemures" were the dead spirits who were said to stare at the living with great shining eyes.

Sportive lemur

The sportive lemur grows up to 24 in. long—just under half of this is tail—and weighs up to 2 lbs. The body is slender, the head is rounded and the snout pointed and rather short. The species is usually divided into six or seven subspecies: five or six forms of sportive lemur, and the weasel lemur. The sportive lemur subspecies differ in coloration and occur in forests in different parts of Madagascar. All are tree dwellers and herbivorous, eating mainly leaves and flowers but also taking some fruit. The adults differ from the true lemurs in that they lose their two upper incisors when they are fully grown.

Sportive lemurs are wholly nocturnal and move within their home ranges with powerful leaps from tree to tree. They are strongly territorial, defending their territories by display, a variety of calls, chasing and sometimes fighting. The gestation period of about four and a half months is long for a mammal of this size and reflects the high degree of brain development in the lemurs, as in all the primates.

The single young is born between September and November, during the Southern Hemisphere's spring. The mother tends to carry her offspring clasped in the thick, warm fur on her underside, though she will often leave it clinging to a branch as she feeds. Although the young are weaned at about four months, they will often follow their mothers around for up to a year. They do eventually leave her to become independent, and attain sexual maturity at about 18 months.

True lemurs and gentle lemurs

True lemurs—six species within the lemur family—are active mostly in the daytime (diurnal), although several of the species are also active at night. They are all forest dwellers, and all but the ring-tailed lemur are arboreal, living in trees. The ring-tailed lemur, however, is quite happy on the ground, and often lives in open areas.

ABOVE The population of the brown lemur of Madagascar and the island of Mayotte in the Comoros was about 50,000 in the 1970s, but is now declining.
BELOW The distribution of some prosimians and the tree shrews.

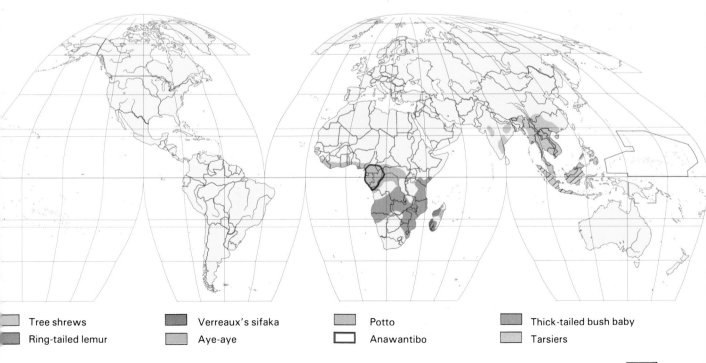

Tree shrews	Verreaux's sifaka	Potto	Thick-tailed bush baby
Ring-tailed lemur	Aye-aye	Anawantibo	Tarsiers

THE RING-TAILED LEMURS
— A CLOSE-KNIT SOCIETY —

The ring-tailed lemur, the least arboreal or tree dwelling of the lemurs, lives in small groups that occasionally combine to form larger bands. The usual group size is about 12, but varies from five to more than 30 individuals. Usually, there is no single leader within the group. The females and males have separate, fairly fluid hierarchies, which are determined by frequent disputes between individuals. These quarrels consist of threats and displays, with occasional bouts of serious fighting.

Female ring-tailed lemurs tend to be dominant over the males and seem to form the core of the social groups, which are made up of a few adult females and their offspring. The males tend not to stick with one group. They leave the troop into which they were born and move among different troops. Females, on the other hand, only leave the troop of their birth in order to start a new troop. This probably accounts for the tendency of the females to dominate the troops, since it is they that define a territory and defend it.

Spreading genes

A biological advantage of the males' habit of roaming is that the troops of ring-tailed lemurs do not become too inbred. There is a good mixing of genes, with successful males fathering young in different troops at different times. Ring-tailed lemurs use a range of calls to communicate, most of which are heard during territorial disputes. When a dispute takes place, groups of females face each other at the edges of their respective territories. The borders are clearly defined, mainly by scent marking. The females then dash at each other uttering a series of cries. The territories are expanded or altered as a result of these ritual interchanges.

The caring lemurs

Usually only one ring-tailed lemur is born at a time after a gestation period of about 130 days. The young may be looked after not only by the mother but by the entire group. Females and their young can often be seen sitting on the forest floor, just grooming and resting themselves, while the young ones scramble from one female to the other, clambering over the indulgent adults.

They can also suckle from any lactating female in the group. This regard for others (or altruism) is part of the complex pattern of social behavior that occurs in many modern-day primates. Ring-tailed lemurs that have been orphaned may be adopted by another female within the group, or even by another group.

Altruistic behavior was, until recently, considered exclusive to the human race. It is, in fact, practiced by many animal species. A female meercat (African mongoose) with young, for instance, is often helped by a young animal from her previous brood. The baby-sitter will care for the young meercats while the mother is out hunting—clearly a sacrifice, since it is unable to go and hunt food for itself.

Such altruism, however, is really a refined form of selfishness. It may appear that the lemur has no thought for its own welfare when it helps another of

its species—using up precious energy and even putting itself at a higher risk of being caught by a predator. But this behavior is actually a quick and efficient way of learning all the skills of parenthood. Although nest or den building and the rearing of young are instinctive forms of behavior, the more experience the animal acquires, the better and more effective a parent it is likely to become.

There is another reason for the lemurs' considerate behavior toward the young of the group. By looking after and protecting the offspring, the adults are helping to ensure that the group's genes are successfully passed on to future generations.

Group life is a useful adaptation: primates, like other social animals, may well find it easier to find and exploit food resources when in a group. Also, the presence of a number of alert eyes and ears helps ensure that predators will be detected before they can attack.

The group is also a vital factor in the learning process of the young ring-tailed lemur. As in all primates, the bond between mother and offspring is especially strong and important; the young animal learns first of all from its mother. As it grows up it continues to observe, imitate and learn from fellow members of the group.

TOP RIGHT Unlike all the other lemurs, ring-tailed lemurs spend much of the time feeding and traveling on the ground. They hunt for insects in the dead wood and termite mounds, but prefer fruit, particularly bananas and figs. The palms of their hands and the soles of their feet are leathery, giving an effective grip on slippery rocks.
RIGHT The ring-tailed lemur can sometimes be found high in the branches of a forest tree, though it prefers broad, horizontal branches to those that are narrow and steeply angled.
FAR LEFT During aggressive encounters, ring-tailed lemurs scent mark their striking black-and-white banded tails and wave them as a defensive gesture at their rivals.

ABOVE Verreaux's sifakas live in small bands, with a similar number of males and females in each group. They eat fruit and leaves as well as bark and dead wood.

BELOW For the first two or three weeks of its life, the newborn ring-tailed lemur is carried clinging to its mother's underside; thereafter it creeps up onto her back.

PROSIMIANS CLASSIFICATION: 1

There are six families within the suborder Prosimii. Four of these are confined to Madagascar and the Comoro Islands: the dwarf and mouse lemurs, the Cheirogaleidae; the lemurs, the Lemuridae; the indri and sifakas, the Indriidae; and the aye-aye, the Daubentoniidae. The other two families have a much wider range in Africa and Asia: the bush babies, pottos and lorises, the Lorisidae; and the tarsiers, the Tarsiidae.

Cheirogaleidae and Lemuridae

The seven species of dwarf and mouse lemurs of the family Cheirogaleidae are scattered around the forests of Madagascar. They include the brown lesser mouse lemur, *Microcebus rufus*; the gray lesser mouse lemur, *M. murinus*; the fat-tailed dwarf lemur, *Cheirogaleus medius*; and the fork-crowned dwarf lemur, *Phaner furcifer*.

There are ten species in the family Lemuridae, and these fall into three subfamilies. They range over most of the forested land in Madagascar and the Comoro Islands to the northeast. The subfamily *Lemurinae*, the typical lemurs, consists of the ruffed lemur, *Varieca variegata*; the ring-tailed lemur, *Lemur catta*—the most common of the lemurs; the black lemur, *L. macaco*; the brown lemur, *L. fulvus*—which is generally divided into seven subspecies; the mongoose lemur, *L. mongoz*; the red-bellied lemur, *L. rubriventer*; and the crowned lemur, *L. coronatus*. The sportive lemur, *Lepilemur mustelinus*, is the only species in the subfamily Lepilemurinae, and the subfamily Hapalemurinae consists of the gray gentle lemur, *Hapalemur griseus*, and the broad-nosed gentle lemur, *H. simus*.

Indriidae and Daubentoniidae

The family Indriidae has only four living representatives: the indri, *Indri indri* (the largest of the prosimians); the two species of sifakas—Verreaux's sifaka, *Propithecus verreauxi*, and the diadem sifaka, *P. diadema*; and the woolly lemur or avahi, *Avahi laniger*. The aye-aye, *Daubentonia madagascariensis*, is the sole member of the family Daubentoniidae. Like the indris it is a forest-dwelling species found only on Madagascar.

ABOVE A sifaka leaps from one tree to another with all its limbs outstretched, but during the last stage of its leap, the animal brings its forelimbs and hind limbs forward so they are at right angles to its body, and comes in to land in an upright position, grasping the tree trunk with both hands and feet.

All true lemurs have long, soft fur and an attractive ruff around the neck and ears. The coloration is very varied and may differ between the sexes. In the black lemur, for instance, the male is an even black color, but the female is light chestnut-brown with a dark face and white ear tufts. The gentle lemurs have small ears, a rounded head, a short snout and short legs. Their teeth are adapted for clamping around bamboo shoots—their staple food—and stripping off the tough outside to expose the tender middle part for eating.

There are two species of gentle lemur. The gray gentle lemur is usually subdivided into three subspecies and mainly occurs in coastal forests and marshes. The broad-nosed gentle lemur lives in an extremely limited area of forest on the east coast of Madagascar; it is very rare and close to extinction.

All lemurs have scent glands, which are used for marking territories. In the ring-tailed lemur, the scent glands are also used to mark the animal's own tail. The banded tail, marked with its owner's distinctive smell and constantly waving about, is used as a means of communication. In the ritualized fights usually associated with territorial disputes, the scent-daubed tail is waved over the lemur's head at its opponent.

Curled up to sleep

The ring-tailed lemur feeds mainly on succulent fruits, but also eats leaves and, very occasionally, insects. It is the only lemur to spend a significant amount of its time on the ground, where it moves as effectively as it does in the trees. Despite this, it does most of its feeding up in the trees. When they go to sleep at night, ring-tailed lemurs curl up like cats so that none of their underside is exposed, and heat loss is reduced to a minimum.

The gestation period in the ring-tailed lemur is long (four and a half months). A single offspring is produced sometime between August and November, and is suckled for about five months. Although sexual maturity is reached at the age of about two and a half years, young males may not be successful at mating until they are older and stronger and can compete with more mature animals.

Ring-tailed lemurs are hardy in captivity and are often seen in zoos. Other lemurs are much more difficult to keep and are rare enough for the

Pen-tailed tree shrew

Potto

Lesser bush baby

Slender loris

Western tarsier

Common tree shrew

744

ABOVE The aye-aye's hand (A) bears a very long, skeletal third finger, which can be used for extracting a larva from a hole in a branch (B). The same finger is used to carry the soft flesh of a fruit to the aye-aye's mouth (C), and to flick up water from a stream to provide a drink (D).

ABOVE The aye-aye also uses its strong, blade-like incisor teeth (that grow continually like those of rodents) to dig out insects from dead bark.

PAGES 746-747 The slow loris of Indonesia and South-east Asia uses its hands to capture insects and often raids birds' nests for eggs and nestlings.

UNDER THREAT

THE LEMURS

The list of endangered species among the lemurs of Madagascar makes one of the most depressing roll calls conservationists can recount. Of the 22 species, all but a few are now considered under threat, and if clearance of their habitat continues unabated, the entire group may soon slide toward the brink of extinction. Several species are already close to that position.

The red-bellied lemur once occurred throughout the rain forests to the east of the island, but it has already become extinct over much of that range. The hairy-eared dwarf lemur has become so rare that the only occasion on which it has been found this century was in 1965. Another member of its family, Coquerel's mouse lemur, is in grave danger because of destruction of its dry deciduous forest habitat in the west of the island. The aye-aye has declined to a remnant population thinly scattered over northern Madagascar; the only living member of its family, the aye-aye may soon lose even that distinction.

In the past, Malagasy natives regarded aye-ayes as bad omens and killed them. Only now, as they and their government become aware of the value of their wildlife, is there any hope for the survival of the great island's prosimians. The one resource that needs protection above all else in Madagascar is its irreplaceable and ancient vegetation. The case of the Madagascan fauna is, sadly, a striking example of how futile it is to provide animals with protection if that does not include conservation of their entire habitat.

ABOVE **Found in Sri Lanka and the south of India, the slender loris usually lives alone or with a mate. Like its relatives, the slow loris and the potto, the slender** loris is nocturnal — hence the large eyes. As it moves through the trees, it always has at least three limbs firmly clamped to a branch for support.

PROSIMIANS CLASSIFICATION: 2

Lorisidae

The family Lorisidae is composed of two subfamilies—the Galaginae and the Lorisinae. The six species of bush babies or galagos make up the subfamily Galaginae. They range over most of sub-Saharan Africa and all are included within the genus *Galago*. The lesser bush baby, *G. senegalensis*, and the thick-tailed or greater bush baby, *G. crassicaudatus*, are usually found in dry habitats. The remaining species, Allen's bush baby, *G. alleni*; the dwarf bush baby, *G. demidovii*, and the two needle-clawed bush babies, *G. elegantulus* and *G. inustus*, all inhabit rain forests.

The subfamily Lorisinae contains the potto, *Perodicticus potto*, which occurs in forests over much of West and Central Africa; the angwantibo or golden potto, *Arctocebus calabarensis*, of equatorial West Africa; the slow loris, *Nycticebus coucang*, of Southeast Asia and Indonesia; and the slender loris, *Loris tardigradus*, of Sri Lanka and parts of southern India.

Tarsiidae

There are three species in the family Tarsiidae, and all belong to the genus *Tarsius*. They live in rain forests, shrubs, and plantations in Indonesia and the Philippines. The Philippine tarsier, *T. syrichta*, occurs in the southeastern Philippines; the spectral or eastern tarsier, *T. spectrum*, inhabits Sulawesi and nearby islands; and the western tarsier, *T. buncanus*, is found in Borneo and Sumatra and their associated islands.

government of Madagascar to prohibit their export—except in exceptional cases for research. As with many other threatened species, however, their survival depends not so much on strict protection as on the protection and survival of their favored habitats. In some cases, short-term survival has been ensured by rearing and breeding in zoos, but captive breeding programs are not an ideal way of conserving species. They can only be a strategy to fall back on as the animals' habitat continues to be destroyed over their natural range.

Sifakas, indris and woolly lemurs

The.e are two species of sifakas: Verreaux's sifaka and the diadem sifaka. Between bouts of feeding, sifakas often sun themselves by sitting on a branch with their arms outstretched. The membrane between their arms and chests increases the area of absorption of the sun's rays. It may be that this sunning position gave rise to the Malagasy tradition (belonging to the natives of Madagascar) that sifakas worship the sun. Another Malagasy legend is that sifakas speed the healing of their wounds by applying herbal remedies.

ABOVE When frightened, slender lorises escape by zig-zagging over the ground and then climbing the first available tree. They retreat slowly up the tree backward, keeping their eyes fixed on the animal that has scared them into flight.

A distinctive feature of the two sifakas is their coloration, which is extremely variable. It ranges from brown or dark red to patched black and white in Verreaux's sifaka, to all white in the diadem sifaka.

The indri has a distinctively patterned white and dark-brown coat. Its tail is only about two inches long. Despite being active during the daytime, the extreme timidity and great rarity of these animals make them difficult to observe in the wild. Their loud calls can, however, be heard. These consist of a long series of cries that act as a means of communication within the groups.

Indris usually live in pairs or in small family groups. They lead a social life with well-organized daily schedules, using customary paths across their group territory. Unless decisive steps are taken to conserve the environment, their distinctive chorus, once a characteristic feature of Madagascan forest life, may well disappear entirely.

The woolly lemur, or avahi, is a nocturnal animal, very little known even to the local Malagasy people. Like the diadem sifaka and indri, it is extremely difficult to keep in captivity. It rests during the day in foliage or in hollow trees in the fast-disappearing rain forests of the island. The woolly lemur's coat is different from that of the sifaka and indri, being thick and woolly (as the name suggests) rather than fine, soft and silky. Its large eyes are more forward-facing than those of the sifakas and indris.

Aye-ayes

The rare, elusive aye-aye is the only living member of its family. It has huge, naked, bat-like ears and long, slender fingers; the middle finger on each hand in particular is extremely long and thin. Unique among primates, the aye-aye's incisors are like those of rodents—they are long and grow continuously, being worn down as the animal eats. Canines are present in young animals but are lost along with the milk teeth.

Aye-ayes have a coarse coat, which varies in color from brown to almost black, and they have a bushy tail. Roughly cat sized, they grown to as much as three feet in length, including the tail, and weigh about four pounds. They are mainly arboreal, descending to the ground only occasionally, and then moving with a clumsy gait. They are also solitary and wholly nocturnal; aye-ayes sleep during the day and emerge to feed after sundown. The daylight hours are spent in a very elaborate nest hidden in the dense vegetation. The nest is made of woven twigs and leaves, with an opening at the side and shredded leaves providing a soft floor for the animals.

The aye-aye has opposable thumbs and long fingers that help it to climb trees, and cling to (and sometimes hang upside-down from) branches. The fingers are also used in grooming. But the thin middle finger has a most unusual use. It is an extremely efficient tool used to extract wood-boring insects and their grubs from burrows deep within rotting branches and trunks. The aye-aye catches larvae in a similar way to the woodpecker. It first taps on the wood with its long middle finger (as a woodpecker does with its beak) in order to pick up the hollow sound of a larval burrow. It then presses its large ear against the surface to listen for the sound of the larvae gnawing the wood. When it locates a grub (or larva), it bites through the wood with its powerful incisors and uses the clawed third finger to pierce and extract the larva.

The aye-aye also feeds on a variety of fruit, including coconuts, using the incisors to penetrate tough husks, and the middle fingers to extract the juicy insides. Aye-ayes live alone or in pairs, and females produce young only every two to three years. The young are born in October or November in the nest. Aye-ayes survive well in captivity, but have never been bred there.

Without doubt one of the rarest and most endangered of all mammals, only a handful of aye-ayes survive in the last fragments of rain forest in the

ABOVE **A young slow loris will cling tightly to the underneath of its mother. Her thick fur coat keeps the body, which has a low metabolic rate, at a steady temperature.**

BELOW **A slow loris moves along a branch in a distinctive spiral fashion to avoid side branches. Unlike the slender loris, it is able to travel along a branch upside-down.**

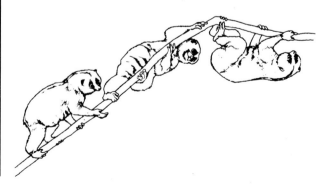

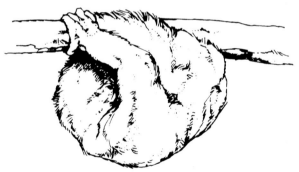

northeast of Madagascar. On an optimistic note, several aye-ayes have been captured in the forests and then freed on the island reserve of Nosi Mangabe off the northeast coast.

Pottos and lorises

The pottos and lorises are compactly built prosimians with rounded heads, large eyes and short, pointed muzzles. The limbs are all about the same length. They have flat nails, except for a claw on the second toe, which is used for grooming the short, woolly fur. Their hands are well adapted to gripping the branches on which they move extremely slowly. The first digit on each hand is opposable and widely separated from the other fingers, allowing it a strong grip.

TOP Apparently headless, the angwantibo of West Africa adopts a defensive position by tucking in its head and presenting its rump to the enemy, which will receive a vicious bite if it gets too close.
ABOVE The potto of the West African rain forests is a strong, muscular animal. The humps on the back of the neck, formed by thickened skin that covers the spinal projections on the animal's vertebrae, form a shield against predators.
ABOVE LEFT The sleeping position of a potto.

ABOVE A baby potto, left on a tree stump, waits for its mother to return from a foraging expedition. For a few days after birth, it is carried clinging to its mother's fur. When it is a little older, the mother will leave it on a branch, well concealed from predators, while she feeds during the night. At daybreak she will collect her young offspring.

ABOVE RIGHT The fingertips of the lesser bush baby have strong, sensitive pads that grip the twigs and branches during the animal's rapid night-time progress through the forest.

The slender loris grows to about 10 in. long, and has a sleek body, long limbs, and great, owl-like eyes. The slow loris grows up to 15 in. long, and whereas the slender loris has no tail, the slow loris has a stumpy tail about 2 in. long. The angwantibo (or golden potto) measures 9-12 in. in length and has almost no tail, while the potto is a little larger with a tail up to 4 in. long.

All the pottos and lorises are omnivorous. Apart from seeds and fruit, insects and insect larvae, they also eat the gum that seeps from certain types of trees. The very slow pace of these prosimians restricts them to eating the insects that no other animals want to eat—foul-smelling insects that do not need to flee predators. In captivity, pottos and lorises have shown they much prefer tastier insects if they are provided.

A distinctive feature of the potto is the presence of long processes (outgrowths) on the upper vertebrae that raise the skin of the back to form bumps. These are covered with horny caps and long, sensitive hairs. Predators are reluctant to attack a bristling ball and the potto can detect any animal sniffing too close to it by the stimulation of the tactile hairs. If a predator does attack, the potto may charge it, with the hard shield to the fore, and deliver a series of vicious bites.

Appealing bush babies

Bush babies are able to leap around at great speed up in the trees. Their attractive appearance, liveliness, and large, gentle eyes help to explain how they came by their name. According to popular African belief, bush babies are the ghosts of dead children.

Of the six bush baby species, the largest is the thick-tailed bush baby, which is about 27.5 in. long, over half of this being tail. The smallest is the dwarf bush baby, which is 16.5 in. long, including 7 in. of tail. Although bush babies eat fruit and gum, they are particularly adept at catching insects. As they move through the foliage, they disturb a variety of insects, which they catch with their hands. The bush baby's large ears and highly developed sense of hearing enable it to react rapidly and accurately. Bush babies can be kept in

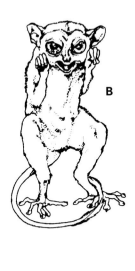

RIGHT **A western tarsier opens its mouth in anger as it is approached by the photographer. Before leaping to another tree, the tarsier can turn its head through almost 360 degrees in order to locate a suitable landing spot. Its ability to do this led to it being hunted by Bornean** head-hunters, who **thought that its head was loose, and the tarsier was used as their totem. Local peoples feared the tarsier, believing it to bring them bad luck.**
ABOVE **The western tarsier in its sleeping position (A), and in its defensive posture (B).**

captivity, but they have the unfortunate habit of bathing their hands and feet with urine—a habit by which they mark their tracks in the wild.

The tarsiers

The three species of tarsier—the spectral tarsier, western tarsier and Philippine tarsier—are similar to each other in size and coloration. Their head and body length is about 5 in., and the tail, which has a characteristic tuft of hair at its tip, is about twice as long. The coat color ranges from slate-gray through brown-gray to a sandy color. The spectral tarsier has furred feet, while those of the Philippine and western tarsiers are naked.

Tarsiers spend most of the day asleep in the vegetation. They emerge in the evening twilight to feed both in the trees and on the ground, preying on invertebrates and occasionally on small mammals, reptiles and birds. Tarsiers usually capture their prey by approaching the victim and leaping on it with great speed and accuracy, killing it with powerful bites. They often then take the food to their perch to eat, holding it with one hand and pulling off pieces, using their teeth rather than their free hand.

The prey is first detected by sound. The tarsier's large, sensitive ears are never still; they are constantly crinkled up and then unfurled as the animal listens to the forest noises. The eyes are huge (each one weighs more than the animal's brain) and face forward to provide binocular vision. Like owls' eyes, the tarsier's eyes are too large to be moved more than a little within their bony orbits (eye sockets), so the animal has to move its head to look around—it can turn its head through almost 360 degrees.

Agile leapers

The tarsier can leap through the branches of trees at great speed, covering distances of several yards without apparent effort. They have strong, long hind limbs—the upper leg is as long as the head and torso combined, and the lower leg and ankle are also greatly elongated. They move so rapidly that people who have seen them in the wild report that they whistle through the air like bullets. However, the noise more probably is due to the tarsier's high-pitched calls. Tarsiers usually have only one offspring at a time. The baby is born with its eyes open and is able to climb immediately after birth.

UNDER THREAT

— TARSIERS AND LORISES —

The three species of tarsiers are all considered under threat. Like most animals of the rain forests, the greatest problem they face is the gradual clearance of their habitat. Since the Philippine tarsier does not occur in any protected areas, this is potentially a problem throughout its range. However, their predicament has been worsened by other pressures. They have suffered from direct persecution in some areas, and where they have colonized plantations they have often been poisoned by dangerous pesticides that are applied to the crops. Tarsiers are also subject to commercial exploitation. They are sold as pets even though they are highly unsuitable for keeping in the home—they are usually infected with parasitic worms that may affect humans, and need to be fed live insects or else they die within a very short time.

The slow loris has been another victim of habitat clearance combined with a variety of other threats over the various parts of its range. In Indonesia, they have been hunted and used in traditional medicine, while in Vietnam, Kampuchea and Laos, years of war over recent decades have destroyed the vegetation in many areas they once occupied. Loss of habitat, once again, has caused the slender loris to decline in India and Sri Lanka. In addition, until recently many of the animals were taken from the wild for use in medicine—both locally, for traditional treatment of eye diseases, and internationally, for modern research.

ABOVE The tarsier's movements are similar to those of tree frogs. In both, the hind legs are very long in relation to the rest of the body. The tarsier derives its name from its elongated tarsi, or ankle bones.

BELOW The tarsier's jumping technique: starting from a vertical position on the tree trunk (A), it turns up to 180 degrees in mid-air (B), to land on a tree trunk with its hands and feet clinging to the tree surface (C).

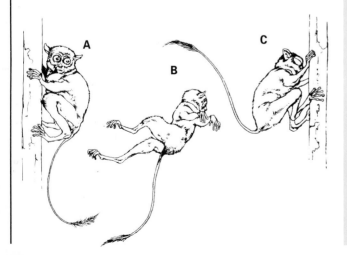

THE PEAK OF EVOLUTION

Monkeys, apes and humans are widely different in their shapes, habits and life-styles—yet they all share a common ancestry and a lively intelligence

The second major group of primates, after the prosimians, is the anthropoids—a group that includes the monkeys and the apes, as well as humans. There are about 145 species of monkeys and apes, and between them they display a great variety of sizes, shapes and life-styles.

Within the group, weights vary from as little as 4 oz. in the pygmy marmoset of the South American forests to over 551 lbs. in the gorilla—an animal that occupies the same type of habitat in Africa. In methods of locomotion there is again great variety. Some species walk on all fours (baboons and gorillas, for example); some can walk upright (humans and, for some of the time, chimpanzees); and some brachiate—that is, they swing along from branches of trees using their arms (for example, gibbons and orangutans). Some anthropoids have a long tail, some have a prehensile tail that can be used for gripping branches, and others possess no tail at all.

Features in common

Despite the diversity of forms, there are some characteristics that are common to the whole group—many of them are features that continue and expand upon the evolutionary trends seen in the prosimians. The brain is highly developed, increasingly so up through the group toward humans. The head is usually rounded, and the eyes point to the front giving excellent binocular vision.

The hands and feet of all anthropoids have become adapted for holding and manipulating objects. Such adaptations include the development of sensitive pads on the hands and feet, the flattening out of claws to form nails, and the possession of opposable digits. In humans, however, the feet have become so highly

BELOW Gorillas are entirely vegetarian, eating mainly leaves, stalks, roots, bark, tubers and fruits.
BELOW RIGHT The pygmy marmoset of South America is one of the smallest of all the monkeys, weighing as little as 4 oz.
PAGE 755 A troop of guerezas, also known as magistrate black colobus monkeys, feed on small leaves and buds in their native African woodlands.

adapted to an upright gait that the big toe is no longer opposable. As if to compensate, humans have long, opposable thumbs that can be used with the fingers to provide a gentle or powerful grip. Other higher primates, such as the gorilla, also have well-developed thumbs, but their hands do not have the precision of human hands.

Limbs of all sizes

The length of the forelimbs, in relation to the hind limbs, varies according to the animal's way of life and method of locomotion. The forelimbs of an orangutan, for example, are comparatively long, for it travels by swinging slowly from branch to branch and long arms give it a greater reach. In humans the hind limbs are the longest so as to increase the distance that can be covered in one stride. In anthropoids that walk on all fours, such as baboons, the arms and legs are of similar length, just as they are among quadruped animals in general.

Body hair varies greatly in thickness and coloration from species to species. Many monkeys and apes have hairless areas on their faces, buttocks, and on their genital regions—where the naked skin may be brightly colored and swollen in the breeding season, to act as a mating signal.

Touch and grip

The hands and feet of many anthropoids have hairless palms and soles, to improve both grip and sensitivity. Good grip is obviously important to a tree-dwelling animal, and it means that many objects besides branches can be grasped. The development of sensitive pads on the fingertips is useful for determining the quality of handholds, and has taken on an even more valuable role among more advanced species. Many of these have developed an acute sense of touch, using their fingertips to explore their environment, assess the quality of food, and use tools with precision. In some of the tree-dwelling species, the enhanced sense of touch is also apparent in the hairless tip to the tail. The sensitive tip enables the animal to feel for a nearby branch before wrapping its tail around it.

The teeth of primates are not specialized for any one food source and are typical of those of omnivorous mammals—those that eat both plant and animal material. However, different species have evolved

TOP AND ABOVE With their large, forward-facing eyes and short snouts, the anthropoids, such as the colobuses of Africa (top) and the squirrel monkeys of Central and South America (above), have flat faces showing distinctly human characteristics. Sight is the most important sense for the monkeys and apes. Compared with most other mammals, the part of their brain that is concerned with vision is particularly enlarged.

ABOVE AND ABOVE RIGHT The marmosets and tamarins are among the most flamboyant and attractive of the South American primates, with a colorful array of fringes, manes and crests. Sadly, many species, such as the cotton-top tamarin (above right), are vulnerable to the destruction of their forest habitat, and the lion tamarin (above), the most spectacular of them all, has now been brought to the verge of extinction.

their own variations. The back teeth of the gorilla, for example, are better adapted for grinding than those of humans, for they have to cope with a more fibrous diet. In some species, the canines are surprisingly long and tusk-like; in such cases they are mainly used for defense or intimidation.

The glands in the skin, such as the sweat glands, are particularly well developed in monkeys and apes. The scent-secreting glands, however, are not as important as they are in many mammals. All female monkeys and apes have two mammary glands, located like human breasts on the females' chests.

One obvious feature that distinguishes the anthropoids from all other mammals is their great range of facial expressions. The range depends in part on the development of a sophisticated set of facial muscles, but the muscles would be of little value without the precise control provided by a large brain. The combination of muscle and brain power has enabled the primates to develop a wide variety of subtle expressions. They are used alone as a means of nonvocal communication—such as a smile or a grimace—or in combination with vocal sounds in the more highly evolved species.

Vocal expression is itself an important feature of the primates, for they all possess a larynx—a box-like enlargement of the windpipe in the throat that contains vocal cords. The cords—thin bands of elastic tissue formed from the lining of the larynx—vibrate in the airflow through the windpipe and produce noise. Muscles in the throat and mouth then modify the noise into the variety of sounds that, in humans, are the basis of language.

Sensory development

A remarkable feature of primates is their excellent color vision. Most mammals see only in black and white, but the primates are all able to perceive color. (They are not unique in the animal kingdom, however—most birds have good color vision and some insects not only possess color vision but also have the ability to perceive ultraviolet light.) The forward-facing eyes

of anthropoids also provide them with excellent binocular vision, giving them an accurate three-dimensional view of the world. The enhanced sense of sight has reduced the importance of scent detection. Consequently, anthropoids tend to have a less acute sense of smell than most other mammals. This is apparent from the shape of a typical monkey's head compared with that of a dog. The monkey has a much flatter face, with a shortened muzzle and larger eyes.

As the sense of smell has declined, the parts of the brain concerned with decoding scent signals have reduced in size, while the parts associated with vision have become more complex. The total brain weight of anthropoids shows a steady increase with evolutionary development, from monkeys through apes to human beings. The increase in the weight of the brain is matched by an increase in surface area—the outer layers of the brain become more and more folded so that a great deal of surface nerve tissue is contained within the confined space inside the skull. Since the brain of a mammal is fully developed at birth, the gestation period of monkeys and apes is prolonged to allow the preparation of their extra-large, complex brains to be completed in the womb.

High society

The comparatively high intelligence of the apes is demonstrated by their complex social life. One measure of the complexity can be seen in their breeding behavior, which is determined less by instinct and environmental conditions than by social interaction. Instead of mating with any animal of the right sex that happens to be receptive, the higher apes seem to take care over choosing a partner, and in many cases form long-term relationships. In this respect, humans differ very little from their near relatives among the great apes.

The more highly evolved the species, the less influence hormones have on the timing of breeding

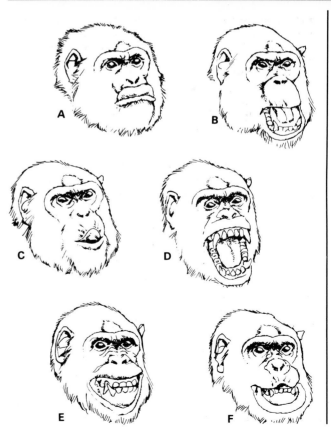

TOP RIGHT Unlike most mammals, advanced anthropoids like the chimpanzee have mobile, expressive faces that allow them to communicate subtle degrees of emotion.
RIGHT The drawings show various expressions in chimps: aggression (A); a playful expression, often accompanied by laughter (B); a chimp making contact with another by hooting (C); a howl of fear or intense emotion (D); a sign of alarm (E); and a female calling to her young (F).

activity; in some cases the animals may mate at any time once they have reached sexual maturity. Females are still dependent on a regular cycle of fertility, and in the case of humans, for example, ovulation takes place once every four weeks. Fertilization can take place only on certain days of the cycle, but some apes will mate regardless of the likelihood of conception. The main reason for this is probably social—mating reinforces the bond between male and female, ensuring that the family group stays together throughout periods of temporary infertility.

Clans and harems

Some species, such as the gorillas, form harems containing one male and several females. Such a system increases the competitive pressure on males, and natural selection has favored males that are large and powerful enough to hold their own against rivals. As a result, males tend to be bigger than females, with more highly developed weaponry in the form of longer canine teeth. They also bear a variety of ruffs and manes to give them a more imposing appearance. In species such as the chimpanzee, groups of males form single-sex clans and mate with similar groups of females. Although there is rivalry between clans, the advantages of individual strength are not as clear-cut as they are in harem-forming species. Among chimpanzees, therefore, there is little size difference between males and females.

Today all the anthropoids are under threat to varying degrees. They are particularly vulnerable to the destruction of the tropical rain forests, and the populations of many forest-dwelling species have been reduced to a dangerous level. It seems almost certain that several will become extinct in the wild in the near future, and while captive colonies may preserve such species, there will be little future for the animals if their natural habitats have been destroyed. It is now up to the most advanced of the anthropoids—human beings—to ensure that the reckless destruction of these wild places does not continue unchecked.

TOP LEFT AND LEFT Infant monkeys and apes are highly dependent on their parents. The adults both provide basic needs such as food (as in the suckling baboon, left) and teach the young the techniques of foraging and movement among the trees (as in the orangutans, top left). The young animals also learn a great deal by playing with other youngsters, often copying the behavior of adults as they play.

FOREST ACROBATS

The monkeys of the New World include some of the most diverse and colorful of primates, such as the howler and spider monkeys and rare golden lion tamarins

Night monkey

Yellow-handed titi

Brown capuchin

Squirrel monkey

Humboldt's woolly monkey

Black spider monkey

Red-handed howler

There are over 130 species of monkeys, distributed over Africa, India, Southeast Asia, Indonesia, Central America and South America. They are commonly divided into two groups, the Old World monkeys (of Africa and Asia) and the New World monkeys (of Central and South America). Separated by geography, these two groups have developed independently from common ancestors—most likely from an extinct family of prosimians. The South American monkeys are probably descended from North American animals that have since disappeared, while the African and southern Asian species appear to have originated in Europe. The move south by monkeys, and the extinction of their North American and European forerunners, can be explained by the climatic changes that were occurring in the early Tertiary period, from about 60 million years ago. During that period the tropical climate that once existed over northern Europe and the central regions of North America gradually gave way to the cold-temperate climate experienced there today. As the climate cooled, so the monkeys spread south.

New World monkeys

The monkeys of Central and South America include the capuchins, sakis, uakaris, howlers, squirrel monkeys, spider monkeys, marmosets and tamarins. One way in which all of these monkeys can be distinguished from their Old World cousins is by the shape of their noses. An African monkey's nostrils are narrow and close-set, rather like a human's, and have only a thin partition separating them. By contrast, those of a South American monkey are widely spaced and are completely separated, with a flat area between them. All the New World monkeys are tree dwellers. In some ways they are more primitive than Old World

BELOW Young night monkeys or douroucoulis stay with their parents for two and a half years before striking out on their own. Here two young animals sit tight between their mother and father—only one offspring is born each year, so the larger youngster to the right must be at least a year older than its sibling. PAGE 761 **Huge eyes provide night monkeys with excellent nocturnal vision, enabling them to leap from tree to tree and catch insects on the darkest nights.**

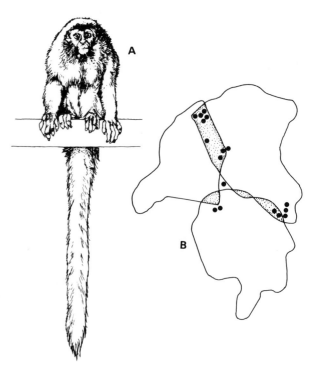

ABOVE **The dusky titi is the most widespread of the titi monkeys. Unusually, it is the male that takes on most of the responsibility for protecting and grooming the young.**
ABOVE RIGHT **A titi monkey at rest in characteristic pose (A). The map (B) shows how the adjacent territories of dusky titis may overlap; the dots indicate the typical positions at which individuals challenge one another during boundary disputes.**

monkeys; their thumbs, for example, are not as opposable (able to be pressed against each of the fingers), so their dexterity is limited. However, several species have become highly specialized for their way of life; the capuchin, howler, woolly and spider monkeys, for instance, all have prehensile tails that give them a great advantage in moving through the trees.

There are two families: the capuchin-like monkeys, which include animals as diverse as the large, powerful howler monkeys and the delicate squirrel monkeys, and the marmosets and tamarins. Many species of capuchin-like monkeys are very closely related, and they often interbreed in captivity. (In general, animals of different species either do not interbreed at all, or, if they do, produce only sterile offspring.) In the wild, the various species of closely related capuchin-like monkeys are isolated from each other by large rivers. The rivers represent insurmountable barriers between different areas of the forest, and as a result interbreeding between the various species is almost unknown.

Foraging by moonlight

Of the capuchin-like monkeys, the most surprising must be the night monkey or douroucouli, the only species among all the monkeys to have become adapted to a nocturnal life. The main advantage of being active during the night is that the animal avoids the day-flying birds of prey that are its main enemies. Its large bulging eyes enable it to see easily in the darkness of the forest. It is a fairly small monkey, with a body some 10-18 in. in length and a 9-18 in. tail. It has a distinctive coloration, with gray upperparts, white eyepatches ringed with black, and a bright orange belly.

Although night monkeys live largely on fruit, they are skilled hunters, capturing insects and occasionally even birds and lizards. They quickly dispatch their larger prey with ferocious bites and pull them to pieces before devouring them. Found in forests throughout much of South America, they live in small family groups consisting of a female, a male, and young of up to two and a half years of age. The family groups forage within a territory of about 25 acres in

size. Neighboring familes may fight if territorial boundaries are breached, but usually disputes are settled with an exchange of whooping cries followed in most cases by the retreat of the intruders.

Leaping monkeys

Near relatives of the night monkeys, the titi monkeys are one of the many kinds of capuchin-like monkeys whose classification is still under debate. Some zoologists consider that there are three species, some four, some five—and these have been further subdivided into 20 or more subspecies. The problems are twofold. As is often the case with equatorial and tropical animals, they live in remote, isolated populations, and they have been little studied in the wild. Since coat colors and habits often vary from place to place among animals of the same species, it is difficult to define the exact status of an animal without prolonged study. The other problem is one that complicates the classification of the whole family. Some apparently different animals can interbreed, yet other animals, some of which appear to be similar, have never had the test of interbreeding applied to them, since they have never been kept in captivity and live in separate areas in the wild.

The coat colors of titi monkeys are variable, even within a single species, and seem to be determined by the dominant colors present in the animal's environment. This suggests that the main purpose of the color is to provide camouflage to conceal the monkeys from the eyes of large birds of prey such as ornate hawk eagles and harpy eagles—their main enemies. Despite the need for camouflage, titi monkeys all bear a distinctive pattern of facial markings accentuated by a ruff of contrasting color and bushy "side-whiskers." Studies of animals in captivity indicate that these features act as signals for individual recognition. Titi monkeys can also express their moods by fluffing up their ruffs and whiskers. Their fur is thick and silky for protection against the chill of the night; without this coat they would lose

ABOVE RIGHT A striking buff tail tip betrays the identity of a dusky titi perched in the forest branches.
RIGHT A male white-faced (or Guianan) saki—the female lacks the dramatic white mask.

PAGES 766-767 A group of red howlers make good use of their prehensile tails as they climb through the branches. Able to curl around and grip branches, the tails act as flexible "fifth limbs."

ABOVE Looking old before its time, a bald, stooping red uakari (pronounced wakari) makes its way along a branch—even young animals have bald heads and move about in a ponderous manner. The pink skin on the head turns bright scarlet when the animal is aroused, but fades from its normal color if the uakari is confined indoors out of the sunlight.

BELOW The two maps indicate the distribution of some of the New World monkeys, in Central and South America.

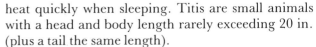

heat quickly when sleeping. Titis are small animals with a head and body length rarely exceeding 20 in. (plus a tail the same length).

Like night monkeys, titis consume a range of food; they eat mainly fruit, leaves and insects, but they also hunt for aquatic prey such as crabs and small fish. A broad diet is essential for their health; titi monkeys cannot survive on plant food alone, for their stomachs are not suited to the digestion of large quantities of plant matter. Titis occur in low-elevation forests, and usually live in shrubs and young trees no more than 33 ft. tall, rather than the high forest canopy.

Sounding off

Titi monkeys live in small family groups of from two to seven animals, usually consisting of an adult pair and their sub-adult offspring of current and previous years. Each group lays claim to a small area of the forest, and reinforces that claim at dawn every day with a prolonged bout of calling. The calls are complicated sequences of bird-like cries, gobbling noises and pumping sounds. As one group stops calling, another starts up, so the forest may echo with the calls for an hour or more every morning. Dusky titis move to their territorial boundaries and often confront neighboring families with displays of their calling power, but other species are normally content to advertise their presence from a distance. For the rest of the day the titis keep quiet, moving through the branches with a stealth that makes them difficult to track.

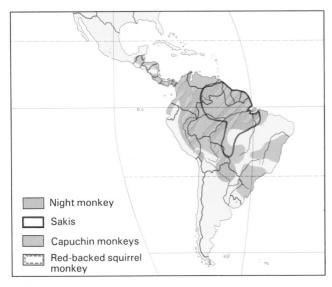

- Night monkey
- Sakis
- Capuchin monkeys
- Red-backed squirrel monkey

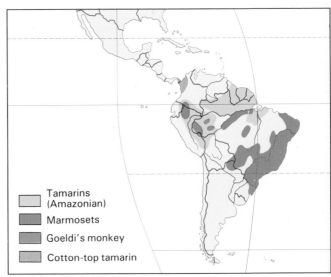

- Tamarins (Amazonian)
- Marmosets
- Goeldi's monkey
- Cotton-top tamarin

ABOVE Sakis make brief foraging visits to the forest floor if there is no danger present. Here a bearded saki moves over the ground, its bushy tail held aloft.
ABOVE RIGHT The red uakari is often kept as a pet by South American Indians.

They capture the monkey by shooting it with an arrow from a blowpipe. The tip of the arrow is dipped in a weak solution of curare—a tree resin made into a poison. Since the solution is weak, it immobilizes rather than kills the animal.

Members of the family move around as a unit, stopping at intervals to groom one another and rest. At night the mother, father, and young all sleep together on the same branch, huddled together for warmth with their tails entwined. Since titi monkeys are monogamous (the adults form stable pairs), males and females form a strong bond, and the males are more closely involved with the care of their offspring than the males of polygamous species (animals that have a number of partners).

Most male primates that live in small groups are tolerant of their offspring and may even play with them for short periods, but among the titi monkeys the male spends more time with the infant than even his mate. He grooms the young animal, plays with it, protects it from enemies and adverse weather conditions, and carries it from tree to tree on his back. His attentiveness continues until the young monkey becomes semi-independent at the age of about four to five months and no longer needs to be carried.

Sakis and uakaris

The sakis and uakaris look quite different from the titi monkeys. They have long hair that makes them appear heavily built, and some species have long beards that they spend much time combing and grooming. They also have opposable thumbs and big toes, which give them a much better grip when they are climbing through the branches.

Although the various species of sakis and uakaris differ greatly in appearance, they all share certain behavioral traits. They live in the treetops in tropical forests, often showing a preference for the humid

THE SQUIRREL MONKEY
— COMMUNES IN THE CANOPY —

The squirrel monkey is a small animal, from 10 to 14.5 in. long with a tail measuring 14.5 – 18.5 in. Widespread throughout Central and South America, it is a social, polygamous species that normally travels around in large, noisy groups. Despite their noisy activity they are elusive creatures since they hardly ever descend toward ground level. Instead, they spend practically all their lives in the upper branches of the very tall trees found in tropical forests. They move from place to place across the forest canopy, continually searching for food that ranges from soft fruit and insects to birds' eggs and small vertebrates such as tree frogs.

The large groups of squirrel monkeys—those in the vast forests of the Amazonian basin may number several hundred individuals—require a complex code of behavior to reduce strife and keep the group together. The average group consists of a dozen or so females in breeding condition and their young, together with a smaller number of adult males. The females coexist amicably, but tend to be intolerant toward males that stray too close; the males on their part keep clear for much of the year, although they remain part of the feeding group, foraging at some distance from the females. The animals use a wide vocabulary of gestures, postures and sounds to communicate their intentions, warn of possible danger, and inform each other of potential food sources.

One curious feature of the behavior of squirrel monkeys is their habit of spreading urine all over their bodies, especially over their tails. A similar custom has been observed among capuchin monkeys. The reason for this self-anointing is not clear, but it could be a form of defense against insects such as mosquitoes and gnats that are not just a nuisance but are also carriers of disease. The urine spread over the animal's body could also act as a scent mark, enabling other members of the group to follow it through dense woodland. Despite this habit, squirrel monkeys are extremely clean and do not have a particularly unpleasant smell.

Too much to eat

Although they inhabit an area with practically no seasons, squirrel monkeys observe annual cycles of behavior. For example, they all mate within a few days of each other, and this results in births occurring at the same time throughout the group. There is no environmental advantage in this as there is among species that live in areas of

LEFT Inquisitive and enterprising, squirrel monkeys have all the agility and swiftness of their namesakes, the squirrels. They use their short, powerful hind legs to leap from branch to branch in search of fruit and insects. **ABOVE RIGHT** Some zoologists consider there to be two separate species — the red-backed squirrel monkey of Central America (left) and the common squirrel monkey of northern and central South America (right). Others, however, class them merely as subspecies of the same animal. **FAR RIGHT** The nimble squirrel monkeys can reach food that is inaccessible to larger, clambering monkeys such as sakis and howlers.

seasonal shortage, so it seems probable that it is a defense tactic. By producing all their young at once, the mothers present potential predators with an overabundance of prey. Since the predators can only eat a limited number of the young at any one time, most survive. By the time the predators are hunting again, the young are learning to look after themselves.

During the breeding season the males in a group may fight among themselves for access to the females. Since the females may mate with several males, no parental bond is formed between the sexes, and the mothers are left almost solely responsible for the care of their offspring. However, within a month or two of birth the young monkeys start play activities with others of their own age. They spend their time in almost continuous play and, in the process, learn how to communicate, find their way about and catch food.

areas near swamps. The air is usually saturated with moisture in these areas, making breathing difficult, so the nostrils of many species are adapted to filter out some of the water and prevent it from clogging the airways of their lungs. The long hair protects the monkeys' bodies and limbs from the frequent, and often torrential, rain that falls on the tropical forests.

Joining up

Sakis and uakaris live in small family groups, but these sometimes join up to form larger aggregations, especially if there is a sudden glut of food in a certain area. Their diet is mixed, but each species has its own preferences; bearded sakis, for example, feed mainly on seeds, which they lodge in a special gap between their teeth and then split open.

Other food eaten by sakis and uakaris includes leaves, flowers, berries, nuts, fruit, honey, insects, and even small birds and mammals if, for any reason, they need extra protein. The mammals that are caught include mice and bats—white-faced sakis have been seen to take bats from hollows in trees. The method of consuming small mammals and birds is rather gruesome—the monkeys tear the prey apart with their hands and then skin the pieces before eating them. To drink, sakis dip their hand into a forest pool or river and then suck the water from the long hairs.

The sakis and uakaris are strong animals, able to make enormous leaps from branch to branch and often across watercourses. Despite their strength, they are not agile when climbing the trees, and move up and down so cautiously that they frequently seem almost clumsy in their movements.

The red uakari is a strange-looking animal. It has long, thick, white or chestnut fur on its body, but its head is almost bald, giving it a rather diseased, aged appearance. It has a red face that turns bright scarlet when it is excited, adding to its bizarre appearance. The red uakari and the black uakari are the only short-tailed species among the New World primates.

ABOVE LEFT AND LEFT In proportion to its body size, the brain of a squirrel monkey is bigger than that of a human. However, a large portion of the brain mass is devoted to the sense of sight, which is particularly acute in squirrel monkeys. Moreover, the surface area of the monkey's brain is relatively small—it is not highly folded like a human brain—so it has much less of the surface nervous tissue that humans use in thought processes.

Squirrel monkeys

Although the chimpanzees and gorillas are commonly considered to be the nearest to man in terms of intelligence, the mental capacity of monkeys is also impressive. Squirrel monkeys do not have such near-human characteristics as chimps and gorillas, but they show their intelligence in other ways: in their adaptability and resourcefulness, and in the complexity and subtlety of their social life.

Squirrel monkeys have also been given the somewhat macabre name of death's-head monkeys, owing to the curious markings on their faces. They have dark muzzles and dark eyepatches, surrounded by a white mask that bears some resemblance to a skull. Their bodies are covered in yellowish green fur fading into red on their lower limbs, and they have long, partly prehensile tails.

Squirrel monkeys are distributed over a large area that includes the most southerly part of Central America and much of South America from Guyana to Bolivia and the basin of the Rio de la Plata in northern Argentina. They are particularly agile monkeys, continually running and leaping from branch to branch. They live in scrublands, mangrove swamps, and moist tropical forests, usually in groups of up to 40 or so individuals.

ABOVE The capuchins are among the most intelligent and resourceful of all the monkeys. They are able to use tools, learn from their successes and failures, and pass on information to others. They also have a complex social life, with a well-defined hierarchy and a sense of collective responsibility—if a young capuchin becomes separated from its parent it is comforted and cared for by the other adults in the group.

Capuchin monkeys

The capuchin monkeys consist of at least four species distributed throughout most of tropical Central and South America: the brown capuchin, white-faced capuchin, and white-fronted and wedged-capped capuchins. They are most common in the hot, humid forests of the great river basins and are often found in the swampy areas and mangrove forests on the river margins. But they also live on seashores and, at the other extreme, in wooded areas of the Andes up to over 8200 ft. above sea level. Of the four species, the brown capuchin is the most widespread; its range overlaps with the ranges of the other three, which rarely if ever encounter one another in the wild.

Capuchins measure 12-22 in. in length, and have a long tail that may be 12-22 in. long. All four limbs are more or less the same length. They get their name

CAPUCHIN-LIKE MONKEYS CLASSIFICATION

The capuchin-like monkeys form the family Cebidae—one of the two families of New World monkeys in the suborder Anthropoidea. There are some 30 species grouped into 11 genera—although the details of classification are subject to constant revision as new facts are brought to light.

There are four species of capuchins proper in the genus *Cebus*, including the brown capuchin, *Cebus apella*, found over much of South America, and the white-face capuchin, *C. capucinus*, of Colombia and Central America. There are also four species of sakis in the genus *Pithecia*, including the white-faced or Guianan saki, *Pithecia pithecia*, of northern Amazonia. A further species of saki belongs to the genus *Chiropotes*: the bearded saki, *C. Satanus*, which inhabits the forests of eastern Amazonia.

Up to six species are recognized in the genus *Alouatta*, the howler monkeys. The Mexican howler, *A. villosa*, and the mantled howler, *A. palliata*, both occur in Mexico and Central America, with the mantled howler spreading into northern South America. The red howler, *A. seniculus*, occurs in northern South America and Amazonia. Four species of spider monkeys belong to the genus *Ateles*, including the black spider monkey, *Ateles paniscus*, and the long-haired spider monkey, *A. belzebuth*, both of which inhabit the Amazon rain forests.

There are three titi monkeys in the genus *Callicebus*, of which the dusky or red titi, *C. moloch*, is the most widespread, occurring over much of Amazonia. The genus *Lagothrix* consists of two woolly monkeys, including Humboldt's or common woolly monkey, *L. lagotricha*, which is widely distributed over the Amazon Basin. Another genus with only two species is *Cacajao*, the uakaris; the red uakari, *C. rubicundus*, inhabits the forests of western Amazonia.

The remaining members of the family are each the only members of their genus. They are the night monkey, owl monkey, or douroucouli, *Aotus trivirgatus*, which occurs over most of South America; the squirrel monkey, *Saimiri sciureus* of both Central and South America; and the muriqui or woolly spider monkey, *Brachyteles arachnoides*, which lives in southeast Brazil.

ABOVE Capuchin monkeys have a bad reputation for they have learned how to take advantage of the activities of farmers and fruit growers, and sometimes descend on crops just as they ripen. BELOW A male capuchin may curl his tail around his body when he is courting a female.

from the curious arrangement of hair on the backs and tops of their rounded heads that forms a dark cap rather like the cowl (or hood) of a Capuchin monk—in pronounced contrast to their almost hairless faces.

Brainy primates

Like the squirrel monkeys, the capuchins have very large brains for their body size. They are probably the most intelligent of the New World monkeys, though not as intelligent as the apes of the Old World. They are also among the easiest to keep in captivity. For this reason much of the information about capuchins was, until recently, derived from captive specimens. Thanks to the efforts of field zoologists, however, this situation has been remedied, and a good deal is known about the life of capuchin monkeys in the wild.

A capuchin's day in the tropical forest begins at dawn, when the troop members awake and start their chorus of loud whistles and hoots. These calls advertise the troop's presence and warn off any competing monkeys that might be tempted to muscle in on the capuchins' feeding grounds. The calls are also used for communication and recognition, and to avert attack from dominant members of the group; young capuchins, for example, will often react noisily to adults who try to steal their food.

ABOVE A group of red howlers howl in unison, releasing one of the loudest sounds produced by any member of the animal kingdom. The main purpose of the calls is territorial; by howling each morning, and as they move to new feeding grounds, a howler troop warns other monkeys of their position and forestalls physical competition for food. PAGES 776-777 Among the high branches of a Venezuelan rain forest, an adult female capuchin (right) and a juvenile male (left) bare their teeth in an aggressive display.

On the march

Because food is normally plentiful in the forest, the capuchins rarely have to travel far to find it, and many groups spend all their time within a small area of a few hundred square yards. Creatures of habit, they tread and retread the same pathways among the densely woven vegetation. As they move around in search of food, capuchin monkeys form a column with older, dominant individuals at the head and subordinate animals following behind. When they are feeding, the dominant male, not surprisingly, takes the richest pickings, but he will share his eating space with favored juveniles and infants.

When foraging, favored females often spread out in front of the dominant male, so that they are the first to find food. But they are also more exposed to attack

ABOVE Like all the howler monkeys, the Mexican black howler of Mexico, Guatemala and Belize relies on leaves to provide at least half of its diet. Leaves are abundant, so there is never any problem with shortages, but since their food value is poor the howlers cannot afford to expend as much energy as other monkeys. They spend a lot of their time asleep, and move slowly through the forest branches with none of the vigor and agility shown by many of the other Latin American monkeys.

from any predators that may be lurking nearby. Low-ranking animals tend to trail behind, gleaning what they can; although they, too, are vulnerable to attack, they dare not risk the wrath of the dominant male by encroaching on his patch.

Battling capuchins

Despite the apparently selfish attitude of the dominant monkeys in the group, individual members will not hesitate to inform the others of a particularly fruitful food source. They do this by using a series of loud, distinctive whistles that bring the others clambering over to share in the feast. Occasionally, the announcement attracts other capuchins in the vicinity—a situation they do not tolerate. The two groups launch into a battle that is invariably won by the largest group, which takes over the tree while the intruders retire in disarray.

Oddly enough a group of capuchins will readily accept a group of squirrel monkeys on their tree, and the two species have often been observed moving about together. The benefits are obvious for the squirrel monkeys: the capuchins have an intimate knowledge of their small territories, and lead the smaller, more wide-ranging squirrel monkeys to the best fruit trees.

Capuchins share with squirrel monkeys the odd habit of spreading urine on themselves. They do not rub it into their fur (indeed, they keep their coats scrupulously clean) but only into their palms and soles. This suggests that its main purpose is to leave a scent track through the branches. It is obvious that, although primates as a whole depend on scent far less than most mammals, capuchin monkeys still use it as a means of finding their way, finding food, and maintaining social bonds.

Measuring intelligence

The intelligence of capuchin monkeys is not as obvious as that of chimpanzees. For example, capuchins in captivity are quite capable of using tools—generally considered one of the prime indicators of high intelligence—yet this behavior has rarely been observed in the wild. The likelihood is that they simply do not need them. This does not denote any lack of intelligence; after all, a philosopher does not use tools, but no one would describe him or her as less intelligent than a carpenter. Since the capuchins

cannot speak to humans it is difficult to assess the power of their logic or imagination; meanwhile the tool-using chimpanzees seem to be more intelligent because they carry out human-type activities in the course of their everyday lives.

Leaf-eating howlers

Although howler monkeys feed on fruit and insects like the majority of New World monkeys, they obtain a large amount of their nutrition from leaves.

Compared with fruit, leaves are very fibrous and low in nutrients, and this makes them hard to digest and unrewarding as a food. Their advantage is that they are plentiful, and an animal that can live on leaves will never starve. Many large hoofed animals such as goats and deer have evolved complex digestive systems to make the most of this abundant food resource; the leaves are fermented in the gut, with the aid of bacteria that break down the fiber and convert it into energy.

Howler monkeys do not have such sophisticated digestive systems, but they do have enlarged sections of the large intestine that contain the necessary bacteria. As a result, the monkeys are able to live for weeks at a time on leaves alone. If fruit is available they

ABOVE Its thick fur silhouetted against the dawn light, a Humboldt's woolly monkey clings to a tree using its strong prehensile tail. Smaller and less acrobatic than the closely related spider monkeys, it avoids direct competition for food and prefers areas that other monkeys rarely visit.

will eat it, but they do not have to rely on it. In practice, they obtain about half their nutrients from leaves, and the remainder from fruit and flowers.

Although the howlers can survive well enough on leaves, they have to be sure they do not use up too much energy. They spend about half their day asleep, and when active they move relatively slowly. They are well equipped for climbing among the branches, for their fully prehensile tails have naked pads on the bottom surface of the end section; these pads are rich in nerve endings like finger pads, to give sensitivity as well as added grip. Howler monkeys are quite heavily built, and their long limbs are very sturdy. Their body length is about 24 in. (females average 20 in.), and their tail length is about the same.

The most striking feature of a howler monkey is its voice. These monkeys are capable of making extraordinarily loud, penetrating calls that are among the loudest produced by any animal. They do this by

ABOVE **Humboldt's woolly monkey has a particularly expressive face—a valuable asset for an animal that lives in social groups of 20 or so individuals, with several mature males in each group. Squabbles over** food **and mating rights are often averted because the monkeys can assess each other's intentions and emotions from their expressions, and so avoid doing anything that might cause an unnecessary fight to break out.**

forcing air through a hole in a bone in the throat (the hyoid bone) that amplifies the sound and makes it audible for about half a mile or more. The males have larger hyoid bones, and their calls are correspondingly louder. The whole sound-making apparatus forms a large Adam's apple, but this is hidden from view by a thick ruff of hair.

The powerful voice turns into a chilling wail when the monkey is fully aroused, but it is normally used to show territorial rights. Like titi monkeys, howlers call at dawn when they wake up and when they move from place to place in the forest. If two groups of howlers approach one another, they launch into a howling duel. The contenders keep their distance, and each monkey simply does its best to out-howl the others. After some time the groups usually back off and retreat in opposite directions.

Howling strategy

It is probable that the howling helps the groups locate and avoid one another, for a confrontation invariably results in a fight, and this is both dangerous and wastes precious energy. For this reason, weaker troops will always try to steer clear of stronger ones. Such behavior also has the effect of spacing troops of howlers throughout the forest so that they all have greater and more equal access to food. The strongest, dominant males are usually responsible for most of the howling and, if necessary, fighting; this conserves the energy of the females, which is more profitably devoted to the bearing and feeding of the young.

Zoologists disagree over the exact number of howler species, some placing all the forms together into one species, others dividing them into as many as six. As a group, they are the most widely distributed of the New World monkeys, and wherever they occur they are often the most numerous. This is almost certainly because their diet allows them to live wherever there are leaf-bearing trees, and in numbers that it would be difficult to support on fruit alone.

The mantled howler has been the most intensively studied. Dark brown or black, mixed on the back with golden hairs, and bearing a fringe of yellowish brown fur on its flanks, it ranges from Mexico through Central America to northern Colombia and Ecuador. The other Central American species is the Mexican howler, which has a completely black, silky coat. The coat of the red howler of north Colombia, Venezuela and the Amazon Basin is variable but tends toward reddish brown, while the black howler, found as far south as Paraguay, varies in color according to sex: males are black, but females are light brown.

Several species among the capuchin-like monkeys have muscular, prehensile tails that can be used to grip branches while their limbs are otherwise occupied. The most highly developed in this respect are the spider monkeys. They also have particularly long forelimbs, and use them to swing through the branches from hand to hand, much like the gibbons of the Old World. It is curious that, despite their similar way of life and the development of their arms, spider monkeys and gibbons have evolved quite different tails. The gibbon's tail is reduced to a mere stump and has no value whatsoever as a means of support. By contrast, a spider monkey uses its long, mobile tail as an extra limb.

FOREST ACROBATS

An extra limb

A spider monkey can swing from a branch, supported only by its tail. It can even use the tail to pluck fruit and carry the food to its mouth. The versatility of this "fifth limb" seems to have reduced the importance of the monkey's hands for holding and manipulating objects. Compared with other species, it has extremely small thumbs—these make it easier for the hand to hook onto a branch and swing without obstruction, but they leave the spider monkey with a comparatively poor grip. As a result, it cannot use its hands with the same dexterity shown by most other New World monkeys.

The black and long-haired spider monkeys have coarse, tousled-looking hair, with coat colors ranging from golden brown to black and tails reaching 35 in. in length. They spend most of their time in the upper branches of the great forest trees, feeding mainly on ripe fruit, leaves and flowers, but also occasionally catching small animals.

Woolly monkeys

There are two species of woolly monkeys, both having soft, dense, woolly fur. Humboldt's woolly monkey is the largest, reaching up to 14 lbs. It resembles a capuchin monkey in many ways, but it has thicker fur and a more protruding forehead. It is the most common species, and ranges over an extensive area of tropical South America, including the upper and middle sections of the Amazon Basin. The second species, the yellow-tailed woolly monkey, has a much more restricted distribution, in the upland forests of northern Peru.

Woolly monkeys normally live in polygamous groups of 20 or so individuals, including several mature males. They feed on ripe fruit and leaves, and

BELOW A black-handed spider monkey on the ground makes a rare sight. Superbly adapted for moving around in trees, spider monkeys spend most of their time high in the forest canopy, searching for fruit. They form small foraging parties, but when danger threatens they may gather together in large groups of 50 or more animals.

ABOVE Perched on a palm leaf, a black-handed spider monkey grasps the leaf stem using its long, opposable big toes that act like the thumbs on human hands. The bright eye rings probably serve as visual signals, enabling the monkeys to keep in contact with one another in the gloom of the dense tropical forests.

ABOVE RIGHT A spider monkey demonstrates the use of the tail as an extra limb. Sensitive and mobile, the tail is strong enough to support the animal's whole weight.

very rarely eat insects or other animals. They are much less acrobatic than the spider monkeys, but possess functional thumbs and are able to make better use of their hands for grasping objects.

Marmosets and tamarins

Of all the New World monkeys, perhaps the most picturesque are the several species of marmosets and tamarins that live in the tropical forests of Brazil and neighboring countries.

Compared to monkeys such as capuchins, these animals are small, ranging from the size of a rat to that of a domestic cat. They have rounded heads adorned with a variety of flamboyant tufts and bristles that give them their names, such as tassel-eared marmoset, mustached tamarin and cotton-top tamarin. Their body hair varies in length, though it is always soft and silky in texture. With the exception of Goeldi's monkey, they have two molar teeth on each side of each jaw, unlike the capuchins (and Goeldi's monkey) which have three.

The hind limbs of marmosets and tamarins are longer than their forelimbs, indicating that they are well adapted for jumping, squirrel-like, from tree to tree; the sharp claws on all their toes (except their big toes) give them a secure grip on the bark when they land.

Until recently, it was thought that marmosets and tamarins were monogamous—having only one mate at a time. New evidence indicates, however, that their mating system can be much more flexible in different

Emperor tamarin

Cotton-top tamarin

White tamarin

Pygmy marmoset

Common marmoset

THE COMMON MARMOSET
— FAMILY TIES —

The common marmoset was known to European naturalists within only a few decades of the discovery of the Americas. In 1551 it was illustrated and briefly, but accurately, described in a book of animals written by the Swiss zoologist Konrad Gesner. He portrayed a small, agile monkey with a mottled grayish brown body, a white forehead and prominent white ear tufts. One of the smallest of all monkeys, typically weighing around 13 oz., the common marmoset soon became a popular pet in South America.

Extended families

Common marmosets live in groups comprising a mature breeding pair, their offspring of preceding seasons, and sometimes one or more adult males that may be unrelated to the other group members. Since they breed fast—in ideal conditions a pair of twins may be born to each breeding female every five months—the family group can be large, with up to 15 individuals. In all cases, the breeding pair are dominant over the rest of the group members.

Although other members of the group may be sexually mature, only one female, the matriarch, actually breeds. She appears to prevent the other females from mating by a combination of visual threats and a form of sexual suppression brought about by chemicals known as pheromones. Pheromones are concentrated in secretions from scent glands, which are detected by other members of the group. In many animals, the chemicals stimulate sexual activity in those individuals that come into contact with them; among female marmosets, however, they seem to do the opposite. Wafts of pheromones produced by the dominant female block the mating instincts of the other females. Subordinate animals must leave the group to start their own families.

Warning smell

The pheromones produced by males have a different function from those of the females. If there is a dispute, a dominant male marmoset will turn his back, fluff up his fur, raise his tail and display his sexual organs to his adversary. The organs are examined and smelled by the subordinate animal, which then usually squeals and flees. The blood of dominant individuals seems to contain a high concentration of hormones linked with aggression. These hormones increase the pheromone level in the secretions produced by the genital scent glands. Warned off by the strong pheromones, the subordinate animal retreats before it becomes involved in

any physical confrontation. In this way, the scent signal acts as an effective method of asserting social status without the need to engage in a fight.

Although the subordinate members of the group are prevented from breeding, they still learn how to care for newborn monkeys. The whole group cooperates to rear and feed the infants, carrying them through the trees and keeping them supplied with insects and small items of food. They also provide both the breeding female, and any child minders that are unable to forage for themselves, with food. Generally the young adults offer their services as child minders, bringing advantages both to themselves and to the group as a whole. The parents can wean their offspring more quickly without abandoning group life, and the young adults serve a kind of apprenticeship in baby care that is invaluable to them when they get the opportunity to claim territories and start breeding themselves.

FAR LEFT Common marmosets are distinguished by tufts of white hairs that grow around their ears.
ABOVE LEFT AND RIGHT Common marmosets are small, nimble primates, rarely exceeding 24 in. in length—of which almost two-thirds is tail. Their size allows them to run along the thinnest branches in pursuit of insects.
BELOW A male marmoset displays to an enemy with his tail raised. Such displays, and the scent signals that go with them, keep intruders at bay and maintain the group hierarchy.

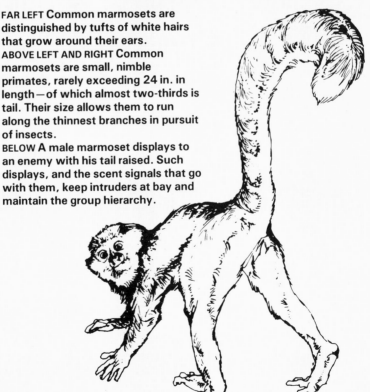

ABOVE **The spectacular golden lion tamarin is one of the rarest of all mammals. It is on the edge of extinction in the wild, with only a few hundred animals surviving in southeast Brazil. They inhabit an area of lowland forest that has been all but destroyed by clearance for agriculture and housing. Fortunately, golden lion tamarins appear to thrive in captivity, and there are now more animals in captive breeding colonies than in their native forests.**

conditions, including monogamy. Unusually for primates, they usually give birth to twins. The parents live with their offspring in family groups, and the male takes an active part in the care of the young. Each group claims an area of forest as its territory or home range, scent-marking the boundaries and warning off intruders by calling and displaying.

All marmosets and tamarins are tree dwellers, and keep to the forests, where the trees themselves, the creepers and epiphytic plants (small plants that take root on the large trees) provide them with plenty of food. Streams or any treeless area can prove effective barriers, preventing movement from one area to another. The resulting isolation of local populations has probably been responsible for the evolution of several species. With no possibility of interbreeding, similar animals in different areas have adapted to local conditions and evolved in different ways.

Attractive in appearance, these monkeys produce musical cries, choruses, and calls that sound very like birdsong—indeed the similarity has been borne out by acoustic analysis. These "songs" provide a particularly valuable means of communication in the forest, for the animals often live amid vegetation so dense that visual communication over distances of more than a few yards is quite impossible.

Dental distinctions

The basic distinction between tamarins and marmosets is to be found in their teeth. Like most monkeys, the tamarins have relatively short lower incisor teeth and long canines. Marmosets, on the other hand, have long chisel-like lower incisors that match their canines. The reason for this is that marmosets use their lower incisors to gouge holes in tree bark, creating a wound for sap to ooze through. The marmoset then licks up the sap. For most species, the sap merely supplements a diet of fruit, flowers and small animals, but for the pygmy marmoset it is an important food; the animal spends well over half its foraging time gnawing holes in bark.

Apart from the tiny pygmy marmoset, all marmosets are classed together in one genus. The common marmoset is probably the best known, with its gray-

ABOVE A black-mantle tamarin marks a branch with the secretion from its scent glands. The scent signals are used to establish territorial rights over a patch of forest, and discourage other tamarins from trespassing.
RIGHT Tamarins and marmosets sport a variety of manes, crests and whiskers; the emperor tamarin has a long, gracefully curved mustache.
PAGES 788-789 Three Goeldi's monkeys cling to a branch in a tangle of lustrous black fur. Rare throughout their range, they have suffered greatly from the clearance of forested land for agriculture.

brown coat and white ear tufts. Like all the marmosets, it feeds on a wide variety of animal and vegetable matter, including the sap of trees, and is widespread throughout northeast Brazil. By contrast, the very rare buffy-headed marmoset is restricted to a few areas of scattered remnant forest on the Atlantic coast of southeast Brazil, and is now on the endangered list. It has grizzled gray and black fur on its back, and thick buff-colored cheek tufts. There are several tufted-ear marmosets, all with long, drooping ear tufts in a variety of colors. They include the black tufted-ear marmoset and the endangered buffy tufted-ear marmoset. All these have dark skin on their faces, but many of the species found in the Amazon Basin—such as the tassel-ear marmoset—have pink faces.

ABOVE With their striking crests of white hair, cotton-top tamarins are one of the most distinctive of the New World monkeys. They are most numerous in areas of forest with thick undergrowth, where they are protected from the sharp eyes of birds of prey.

Tamarins

Like the marmosets, the majority of tamarins are now classed together in one genus. They include the two subspecies of the red-handed tamarin—one with reddish hands found to the north of the Amazon, and one with black hands (despite the name) found to the south of the Amazon. Such variations are typical of the evolutionary divergence brought about by isolation. Several species are adorned with mustaches of variable length; the most spectacular are those of the emperor tamarin, which droop down several inches from its muzzle.

The cotton-top has a particularly striking appearance owing to the shock of white hair that sprouts from the top of its head; it has been called the Liszt monkey because of a fancied resemblance to the Hungarian composer's hairstyle. It is also known as the nightingale monkey—a reference to its bird-like song.

Classified in a genus of their own, the lion tamarins of southeast Brazil are among the rarest of all mammals. Very few remain in the wild—they live in patches of tropical forest and even in cultivated areas. There are three distinct races of lion tamarins, and they are sometimes considered to be separate species. Two of the races have thick golden manes: the golden lion tamarin, which is red-gold all over; and the golden-headed lion tamarin, which is black with a golden mane, rump and thighs. The golden-rumped or black lion tamarin is black with a golden or rusty-colored rump and forelimbs.

MARMOSETS AND TAMARINS CLASSIFICATION

The marmosets and tamarins form the second family among the New World monkeys, the Callitrichidae. There are over 20 species, falling into five genera, and all are native to Central and tropical South America.

Most of the marmosets belong to the genus *Callithrix*, including the common marmoset, *C. jacchus*, of northeast Brazil; the buffy-headed marmoset, *C. flaviceps*, found in scattered locations in southeast Brazil; the black tufted-ear marmoset, *C. penicillata*, of southern Brazil; and the tassel-ear marmoset, *C. humeralifer*, found in Amazonian Brazil. The pygmy marmoset, *Cebuella pygmaea*, is classed in a genus of its own. The smallest of all monkeys, it is found in the upper reaches of the Amazon Basin.

Of the 12 species of tamarin, 11 belong to the genus *Saguinus*. These include the red-handed tamarin, *S. midas*, with two subspecies found either side of the Amazon; the emperor tamarin, *S. imperator*, and the black-mantle tamarin, *S. nigricollis*, both of upper Amazonia; the pied bare-face tamarin, *S. bicolor*, found north of the Amazon; the cotton-top tamarin, *S. oedipus*, of northern Colombia; and the saddle-back tamarin, *S. fuscicollis*, which has a total of 14 subspecies including an entirely pale form known as the white tamarin. Classed in a genus by itself, the lion tamarin, *Leontopithecus rosalia*, is one of the rarest of all mammals; the three subspecies survive in scattered populations in Brazil.

The remaining species, Goeldi's monkey, *Callimico goeldii*, of the upper Amazon, differs in several respects from the other tamarins and marmosets. For a long time it was classed in a family of its own, but it is now included in the family Callitrichidae.

THE VERSATILE TROOPERS

Agile, enterprising and adaptable, the Old
World monkeys thrive in most tropical habitats
and some have found a life of relative ease in
the realm of humans

Crab-eating macaque

Pig-tailed macaque

Drill

Savannah baboon

Celebes macaque

Hamadryas baboon

Gelada baboon

Lion-tailed macaque

Although the New World monkeys have a lot in common with humans, including in some cases considerable intelligence, it is the higher primates of the Old World that are our closest relatives. Apart from humans, the other three families that make up the Old World primates are the great and lesser apes (see pp. 837-890), and the Old World monkeys. The latter are generally divided into two subfamilies: the baboons, macaques and guenons; and the colobus and leaf monkeys.

The Old World monkeys are sometimes called the catarrhine monkeys, a word derived from the Greek and referring to their close-set, downward-facing nostrils—a characteristic shared by man. (South American monkeys do not have prominent noses— they have broadly splayed nostrils with a flat area between.) Old World monkeys share some other features with humans, including a large outer ear with a long auditory canal, and 32 teeth arranged exactly as in humans. They also have a non-prehensile or absent tail (although some species have prehensile tails when they are young).

Often regarded as the "typical" monkeys, the macaques, baboons and their allies are among the most familiar of all the primates, for their habits often bring them into contact with man. They show little or no shyness in human company, and seem happy to live in built-up areas. An example is the rhesus macaque, which lives in semi-domestication within the precincts of temples and monasteries in northern India and Nepal. Many species have learned to take advantage of the activities of farmers and growers, and have discovered the wealth of food to be gleaned from warehouses and garbage dumps.

Old World monkeys vary in size from some 13 in. (head-body length) in the talapoin monkey to over 27 in. in the mandrill. The relative weights of these

PAGE 791 **Old World monkeys** range from tree-living animals such as the colobuses to specialized ground dwellers like the baboons. The vervet monkey, pictured here, is at home in both environments, spending its nights in the branches and searching for food on the ground by day.

ABOVE RIGHT A macaque on the attack: glaring at an enemy (A), baring its teeth (B), and lowering its head before springing (C).
RIGHT The dark, velvety fur of a newborn Barbary macaque contrasts with the long, pale coat of its mother. Macaques retain a close bond with their young, even as adults.

ABOVE **Macaques forage for fruit, young leaves, insects, reptiles and small mammals. Some catch aquatic food, using their** long **tail as a balance when they lean over the water.** BELOW **The distribution of several groups of the Old World monkeys.**

animals show the range more dramatically, with the male talapoins at 3 lbs. or so, and the mandrill weighing some 110 lbs. They all have flat nails on their toes, but they generally walk on all fours. Certain species are able to stand up on their hind legs and walk for short distances, especially when their hands are occupied, but they do not usually do this.

Both the thumbs and big toes of the monkeys are opposable, giving the tree-dwelling species a firm grip on branches, and giving all species a precision and dexterity that comes in useful for grooming and feeding. In tree dwellers, the hind limbs are longer than the forelimbs and are more muscular, giving them the power to leap from branch to branch. In ground dwellers such as the baboons, the forelimbs are the same length or longer to give a less awkward gait when they travel on all fours. They have large cheek pouches that are used to store food, allowing them to forage in haste and eat at leisure.

Many of these monkeys have dramatically colored facial skin, rump patches and genital regions, and the colors often get brighter during the mating season. The genitals of many females also swell when they are in heat. Old World monkeys are polygamous (having more than one mate) and live in social groups based on harems, or large mixed bands. Typically, baboons

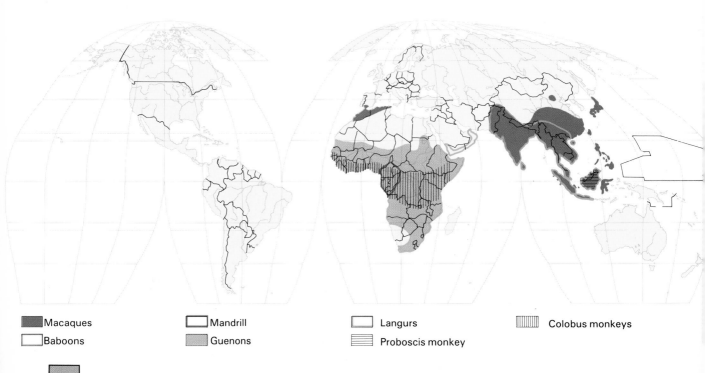

Macaques   Mandrill   Langurs   Colobus monkeys

Baboons   Guenons   Proboscis monkey

and macaques live in troops of up to 50 individuals, but 1000-strong troops of gelada baboons have been recorded. Gestation lasts from 165 to 240 days, and normally only one offspring is born at a time.

Macaques of the Rock

Barbary macaques were introduced to the Rock of Gibraltar for sport during the early 18th century, and they flourished for over two centuries until reduced numbers made fresh introductions necessary in the 1940s. Wrongly, but commonly, called "Barbary apes," these macaques live in two troops of between 30 and 40 animals each. One troop prefers to stay on high ground among the rocks, while the other forages near the road leading to the town where they receive food and much attention from tourists. The British administration on Gibraltar is keen to maintain the colony, partly because of a legend stating that the British will lose control of the Rock if the macaques disappear. Whatever their motives, their concern for the welfare of the colony is welcome, since Barbary macaques are now rare in their native North Africa.

Both the Barbary macaques of Morocco and Algeria and the Gibraltar macaque are tailless and grow to some 24 in. long, reaching a maximum weight of about 33 lbs. They have thick gray-brown fur and a comparatively thick-set appearance, although beneath the fur they are actually very agile and slender. Their fur is good insulation against the cold, for they often live at high elevations in mountainous terrain. Barbary macaques that are kept in zoos and wildlife parks in temperate climates around the world are noted for their tolerance of low temperatures, and they are often found outside in mid-winter.

Macaques are widely distributed over southern and Southeast Asia as well as North Africa. Like the Barbary macaques, the Asian species are much more tolerant of adverse weather conditions than other monkeys and apes, and are able to cope with extremes

RIGHT The various species of guenons avoid too much competition with one another for food by foraging at different levels. The diana monkey (A) and the spot-nosed monkey (B) are found high in the trees and rarely descend to ground level. The mona monkey (C) and the mustached monkey (D) usually keep to branches lower down. De Brazza's monkey (E), the talapoin monkey (F), the vervet (G), and the lesser spot-nosed monkey (H) tend to forage on the ground or among the lowest branches.

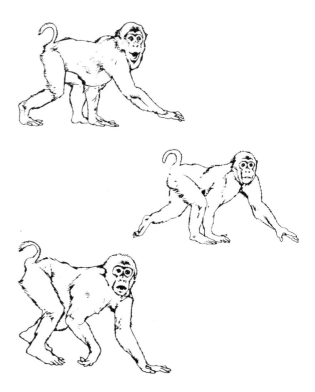

LEFT The naked face of the stump-tailed macaque turns a blotchy brown color when it is exposed to strong sunlight. Stump-tailed macaques occur in forests over much of south China and Southeast Asia, in some areas at elevations of over 7500 ft.
BELOW Macaques walk on all fours, placing the palms of their hands and feet flat on the ground.

— OLD WORLD MONKEYS — GENERAL CLASSIFICATION

The Old World monkeys all belong to one family, the Cercopithecidae—part of the primate suborder Anthropoidea. The family is divided into two subfamilies, both of which occur in Africa and Asia. The macaques, baboons, mangabeys, and guenons are all part of the subfamily Cercopithicinae, which has eight genera and approximately 45 species. The colobuses, leaf monkeys, snub-nosed monkeys, and surelis, on the other hand, belong to the subfamily Colobinae— the colobines—which comprises five genera and a total of over 35 species.

of both heat and cold. The more northerly species grow long hair on their upper bodies to protect them during the winter, and they can often be seen foraging for food when the snow is thick on the ground.

Japanese macaques are still quite numerous on the various islands that make up the Japanese archipelago. The local people have traditionally shown them great respect. The animals that received most attention from the researchers were those living on Koshima in southern Honshu—an island that has become well known in zoological circles.

Status and seduction

In captivity, adult male macaques often reign like tyrants over the monkey communities, presumably because the subordinate individuals have no means of escaping them. Observation of the Koshima macaques

showed that this is not the case in the wild. Older males certainly occupy a higher position on the hierarchical ladder, but they exercise their rights in a much less aggressive fashion.

For the senior males, the main purpose of the hierarchical structure is to ensure that they have rights of access to breeding females. High-ranking males have the first choice during the mating season, but this does not mean that they keep all the eligible females to themselves. In a large community, it is simply impossible for a few boss males to control all the mature females, and as a result several escape their control and mate with suitors of lower rank.

Sometimes a high-status male macaque will attempt to kidnap a female from another male. He may be successful, but quite often the female prefers to stay with the first male, possibly because the pair are genuinely fond of one another. Whatever her reasons, the female generally retreats at the approach of a higher-ranking male or her partner guides her away, as if to remove her from temptation. Surprisingly, these maneuvers do not lead to angry scenes, and encounters between males of different ranks under these circumstances are peaceful.

Although the leader of a troop finds it easy to assert his rights, he rarely holds his dominant position for

ABOVE Although they are mainly forest dwellers, Japanese macaques often forage on the seashore for small animals and edible plant debris. They show a great capacity to learn new ways of dealing with unfamiliar food and to pass on the knowledge to other members of their colony. **PAGES 798-799** Sheltering from the wintry weather, a group of Japanese macaques take advantage of the warmth provided by a pool of water heated by underground volcanic activity.

long. There are always younger or more enterprising males waiting to take his place. Once displaced, the former leader is not always able to revert to a subordinate position in the troop, and some males end up by living apart from the group on their own. This is not always the case, but despite many years of research it has proved impossible to determine why some males and not others leave the group. The character of the animal must be an important factor; in monkeys, just as in man, there are large differences in temperament among individuals.

By studying the behavior of the Koshima macaques, zoologists have obtained proof that animals living in closely knit communities are able to learn from the discoveries made by individuals in the group. Such learning is basic to human civilization, for it enables society as a whole to benefit from the ideas and skills

ABOVE Though rhesus monkeys are one of the most abundant species of macaques, their numbers are declining in many rural areas. Their contact with humans has proved to be a mixed blessing: they have colonized urban habitats and appear to thrive in them, but huge numbers have been caught and kept in captivity, many for use in medical research.

of specialists. Until the research on Koshima island, there was little proof that animal societies could benefit in the same way.

Imo's discovery

In 1953, a researcher described how a female of nearly two years old, who had been given the name Imo, learned by chance to clean sweet potatoes by dipping them in water and rubbing them in her hands before eating them. This discovery gave Imo an advantage over her companions who had to peel the potatoes with their teeth to remove the sand.

A simple enough skill to acquire, Imo's discovery was not particularly remarkable. What intrigued the researchers was the way the habit of washing potatoes before eating them gradually spread throughout one section of the community and then to the entire group—Imo's companions learned the new technique by imitating her actions.

Before Imo's companions took to washing the sand from their sweet potatoes, the ability to promote culture—that is, transmit one's own experience to others within a social context—was thought to be exclusive to humans. At that moment, a barrier that we had placed between ourselves and other animals collapsed, and as a result, we have had to re-examine our relationship with the rest of the animal kingdom.

The researchers made a careful study of the way the community learned Imo's potato-washing technique. The first to imitate her was a friend with whom she played. Then Imo's mother learned how to wash potatoes in the water. At first the knowledge spread among the young macaques who found it easier to learn. The older animals proved extremely slow on the uptake, and only two adult females, apart from Imo's mother, learned the technique. No males over four years old accepted the discovery.

Spreading knowledge

Thirty-five years after Imo's discovery, all the monkeys in Koshima have learned to wash the sand from sweet potatoes. The knowledge spread laterally through the community (among animals of the same age group) and was also passed down from generation to generation. Other techniques have been passed on

in the same way. For example, the Koshima macaques now prefer to wash their potatoes in salt water, probably because the salt water adds extra taste.

They also learned how to clean wheat grains thrown onto the sand by the scientists—another discovery made by Imo. One day she took a handful of the sand and grain mixture and threw it into the water. Once the sand sank to the bottom, Imo scooped up and ate the lighter wheat grains that were floating on the surface. This technique has also been passed on from one individual to another.

In view of these developments, it is not difficult to see how foraging and hunting skills, and eventually tool use and manufacture, could be discovered by one individual and taken up by the rest of the community. From the study of the Koshima macaques we may appreciate the kinds of social interactions and learning that might have powered man's first steps toward developing the high-technology culture of today.

The rhesus monkey, or rhesus macaque, is a sociable animal found from Afghanistan to northern India, Burma, north Thailand, Vietnam and southern China. The male grows up to about 26 in. long, not including the tail, which is half as long again. It is, as with so many of the monkeys, bigger than the female. The coat is dull brown above and pale underneath.

ABOVE LEFT A newborn rhesus monkey clings to its mother, its mouth securely attached to her teat. The young monkey will spend the first few weeks of its life alone with her, watching all that is going on around, before it gradually comes into contact with other youngsters.
ABOVE By observing their mothers' activities and playing with one another, young rhesus monkeys learn the basics of social behavior—including mating behavior and the art of grooming.

Both the face and rump are hairless, and are colored red in the adult.

The rhesus monkey is not only sociable with its own kind—it lives in large groups made up of distinct clans—but it is also tolerant of human company. In many parts of India, rhesus monkeys enjoy considerable protection despite the damage they can inflict to crops. The Indian people's respect for these animals is so deeply rooted that it is sometimes easier to find monkeys of various species in towns and villages than in the wild wooded and rocky areas that were once their main haunts.

The rhesus monkeys' tolerance of humans is the main reason why they are the species of monkey most frequently seen in zoos. Unfortunately for the rhesus, this is also why it has been used in great numbers as a laboratory animal for medical research.

ABOVE With its grayish facial ruff and contrasting black body color, the lion-tailed macaque of southern India is one of the most striking of all the macaques. It spends most of its life high in the trees in its rain forest home, feeding on fruit, nuts, leaves and insects. Though it shares its range with the bonnet macaque, the two species coexist in peace because the bonnet macaque is primarily a terrestrial monkey that forages for food among the leaf litter on the forest floor.

The rhesus factor

It is to the rhesus monkey that we owe the discovery of a blood factor (or element)—also present in human blood—that is extremely important in deciding whether certain blood transfusions will succeed or fail. The rhesus factor, first discovered in 1940 during laboratory tests on the blood of the rhesus monkey, is a protein in the red blood cells capable of stimulating the formation of an antibody in the blood. Five percent of people do not inherit the rhesus factor, and if their rhesus-negative (Rh-negative) blood is mixed with rhesus-positive (Rh-positive) blood, in a blood transfusion for example, a form of rejection may occur.

Pregnant women who are Rh-negative are subject to the greatest risk; if they have an Rh-positive baby, Rh-positive antibodies can travel from the unborn child through the placenta and remain in the mother's bloodstream. If she later becomes pregnant with an Rh-negative baby, the Rh-positive antibodies in her bloodstream can damage the child. The sacrifice of many rhesus monkeys in the laboratory has enabled us to understand this process and thus prevent such complications from arising.

Rhesuses in research

We owe many other important discoveries in the field of human medicine to the huge numbers of rhesus monkeys that have been used in laboratories around the world. The rhesus monkey has contributed to our understanding of our own physiology—the functioning of organs, tissues and cells. However, rhesus monkeys, other monkeys and laboratory research animals in general have often been kept in cramped, unsatisfactory conditions, and the use of animals in laboratory research is now a controversial subject. There is growing public pressure, often supported by scientists themselves, both to find substitutes for living creatures and to see that the live animals that are still used are treated well. There is also an increasing resistance to the use of animals for research into nonessential consumer items such as cosmetics.

Rhesus monkeys are known for their intelligence, which is on a par with that of chimpanzees. Under test conditions they can solve complicated problems and they learn quickly by watching human beings. In the wild, no individual is more important in the rhesus' learning process than the mother.

MACAQUES CLASSIFICATION

The 15 species of macaques all belong to the genus *Macaca*. They range across much of Asia, and one species also occurs in northwest Africa. Their habitats include forests, scrubland, swamps, riverbanks, and the outskirts of human settlements. The Asian species include the Japanese macaque, *M. fuscata*; the rhesus monkey or rhesus macaque, *M. mulatta*, which is widespread across India, Southeast Asia, and China; the toque macaque, *M. sinica*, of Sri Lanka; the very rare lion-tailed macaque, *M. silenus*, which inhabits a small region of southern India; the stump-tailed macaque, *M. arctoides*, of eastern India, southern China, and Vietnam; the pig-tailed macaque, *M. nemestrina*, of eastern India, Southeast Asia, and Indonesia; the bonnet macaque, *M. radiata*, of southern India; the crab-eating macaque, *M. fascicularis,* of Burma, the Philippines, and Indonesia; and the Celebes macaque, *M. nigra,* of Sulawesi. The barbary macaque, *M. sylvanus*, is the only African macaque and is native to Algeria and Morocco; it also occurs in Gibraltar, where it was probably introduced.

ABOVE For crab-eating macaques, like many primates, grooming is one of the most important elements of social behavior, establishing and strengthening relationships within a group. Hierarchical barriers are broken down during the rituals of grooming, and dominant and subordinate animals meet on equal terms—although a longer time is usually spent in the delousing of dominant individuals.

It is from the mother that the young rhesus learns forms of behavior that it will need to survive in rhesus society, a process known as cultural transmission. With the mother the young animal learns to groom and to walk, and with its peers it learns to play.

Testing the bonds

The relationship between mother and offspring during the first years of life is crucially important to the emotional well-being of the young animal. Young rhesus monkeys that have been deprived of the normal maternal affection show abnormal and often delayed psychological development, as well as abnormal social behavior. This was demonstrated in the 1950s by Harry Harlow, an American psychologist who investigated how young rhesus monkeys learned. In the process, he was forced to consider the importance of the mother/child bond.

LEFT The pig-tailed macaque of Assam, Burma, Southeast Asia and Indonesia is declining over many parts of its range. It is hunted for meat and medicinal products, and is killed as a pest on agricultural land.

BELOW LEFT There are several isolated subspecies of the Celebes macaque on the island of Sulawesi. In some areas, the people have traditionally regarded these monkeys as sacred animals.

For his research into learning, Harlow needed a regular supply of infant rhesus monkeys, each of which had the same rearing history. Because mother monkeys are individuals and affect the offspring differently, he removed them just after birth and raised the young in solitary confinement. Deprived of their mothers, the young grew up to be either very aggressive or withdrawn, cried a good deal, and sucked their own fingers and toes. The males grew up to be sexually inadequate, while the females were unwilling to mate and if they gave birth, they did not take proper care of their young.

Harlow showed that one of the elements essential to healthy mental development in a young rhesus monkey is physical contact with its mother—the need to feel maternal warmth—as well as real "mother love." In one of his famous experiments, Harlow removed some rhesus infants from their mothers and offered them the choice of dummy substitutes. One was built of wire with babies' feeding bottles attached to the front; another was made of soft cloth but without the feeding bottles. The rhesus infants used the "wire mother" only for feeding and took refuge with the "cloth mother" when frightened, when demonstrating affection and when sleeping.

As they grew up and were placed with other monkeys, the rhesus monkeys that had been deprived of their real mothers showed disturbed behavior; the longer the time they were kept from their mother, the worse their psychological state became.

Love and confidence

The young clearly require more than just milk from their mothers for their full development. The sense of security afforded by the mother's warm, soft body and her emotional support gives the young animal the confidence to approach new objects and to become involved in situations from which it would run away if it were alone. The bond between the mother and offspring gives the young one the chance to learn

more about the outside world. Harlow's work is relevant to an understanding of human behavior, especially to the great importance of the mother/child relationship in humans.

As well as the rhesus and Japanese macaques, there are another 13 species of macaques. Within the group there are variations in feeding, habitat and behavior. The smallest is the toque macaque of Sri Lanka, females of which may weigh as little as 8 lbs. The largest is the Japanese macaque, which can reach 40 lbs.

All macaques are sturdy-looking monkeys, and the males are bigger than the females. Macaques' coats are coarse and usually a dull brown color, paler underneath. The infants' fur is softer and is often a different color than the adults'. Some macaques, such as the bonnet and toque macaques, have long tails, while others, like the stump-tailed and Celebes macaques, have no tail.

Macaques are active mainly during the day, and partly ground-dwelling, though they spend time in trees and on rocks. Their broad diet centers upon fruit, but also includes insects, foliage, crops and even small animals and birds. While the rhesus lives happily in the company of humans, other macaques are far more shy and retiring. The lion-tailed macaque is one of the rarest of primates and is seriously threatened with extinction by the destruction of its forest home in south India. There may be only a few hundred left in the wild, even though they are protected. Also threatened by loss of their forest habitat, by persecution and by hunting for food and for capture as pets are the Japanese macaque, the toque macaque, and the stump-tailed and Formosan rock macaques.

Another threatened species is the pig-tailed macaque. It bears a strong resemblance to the baboon: the male has long upper canines that it bares during threat displays. Despite their threatening appearance, pig-tailed macaques are not particularly aggressive, and females and young animals are even trained to collect coconuts in certain areas.

TOP AND ABOVE The yellow baboon is a distinct form of the savannah baboon, occurring in lowland regions of East and Central Africa.
BELOW A dominant baboon bares his sharp canine teeth at another male (A). If the challenger does not move, the dominant male advances with stiff legs and his mouth wide open (B). The submissive male adopts the posture of a receptive female to pacify the higher-ranking male (C).

A   B   C

THE SAVANNAH BABOON
— LIFE OF THE TROOP —

Many of the characteristics of baboon behavior may be understood in terms of the savannah environment they inhabit. The most direct ancestors of humans may very well have evolved in just this type of environment, and many biologists have considered the study of baboon behavior to be particularly relevant to the understanding of human behavior and its evolution. Because of this, there is a great amount of information on these primates.

Social groups of savannah baboons consist of a number of adult males, adult females and offspring. There are usually more adult females than males, for two reasons. First, females mature several years before males and thus are counted as adults, while same-aged young males are not. Second, all males emigrate from the group into which they were born into a new group, and they are more subject to injury, predation and disease during this process, which occurs around the time they reach sexual maturity.

Dominance hierarchy

Because females, unlike males, remain in their natal groups throughout their lives, they form close, long-term bonds with close relatives. In this way, the adult females provide a stable core for the entire social group. The group usually moves as an integrated whole, and animals do not split into consistent subgroups or foraging parties. Within the group, the females form a linear dominance hierarchy, or "pecking order." High-ranking females have priority access to preferred resting or feeding spots, receive more friendly approaches, and face less aggression from others. Rank is largely inherited; in adolescence, daughters assume ranks similar to those of their mothers. Although females typically spend most of their time in close proximity to their mothers, aunts, sisters, daughters, and so forth, they also form friendships with non-relatives within their groups who are close in rank, and seek to form bonds with higher-ranking females. Friendships with higher-ranking females possibly aid in increasing access to limited resources.

Relationships among males are more aggressive than among females because the males are unrelated and because they compete within the group for access to females. Males, like females, can be placed in a dominance hierarchy, but unlike the female hierarchy, theirs is less stable and cannot be predicted on the basis of heredity. Male dominance rank is determined by a combination of attributes, including age, size and fighting ability.

A male baboon of low status that challenges one of the dominant males shows defiance by refusing to lower his eyes or by blocking the dominant baboon's path. The latter then tries to outstare the challenger, and if this fails, he will open his mouth wide to display his threatening teeth.

Interestingly, high rank among males does not necessarily confer access to the most females. Instead, factors such as length of time as a member of the group, the presence of allies, and female choice also influence mating success. Males who establish close bonds with particular females throughout the year often gain preferential access to such females when they are in estrus, even if the males themselves are low-ranking. These male-female "friendships" are expressed through time spent grooming one another, resting in close proximity, and occasions when one comes to the aid of the other during squabbles and altercations within the group.

Male savannah baboons do form temporary coalitions to acquire females in heat from other, higher-ranking males. In one group, for example, studied by Barbara Smuts, young adult males (8 to 10 years of age) were dominant to older males (about 13 years of age and older), but during the day older males repeatedly used coalitions with older males to take away consort partners from younger males. Older males also used coalitions to protect their own consortships from younger males. At night, however, when darkness prevented such effective coordinated action, the younger males were able to take females away from older males through individual aggressive action. As younger males aged, they began to adopt the coalition strategy of the older males.

Surviving on the savannah

Savannah baboon troops must spend a large portion of the day traveling over wide areas in order to find enough to eat because they are large animals and eat foods that are scattered in patches. In the arid savannahs of Ambolesi National Park in Kenya, baboons typically travel more than 5 miles per day in search of grass, tubers, bulbs, corms, rhizomes, flowers, fruits, leaves, seeds, tree gum, insects, eggs and even the occassional hare, vervet or infant gazelle. In bad times, however, baboons can subsist entirely on grass and subterranean corms, rhizomes and bulbs.

To successfully inhabit such poor environment as the dry savannah, species must show great adaptability. In the baboon, behavior and feeding habits may vary from troop to troop, as well as from species to species. The rich vocabularly of grunts, barks and other utterances used by baboons—and perhaps even the meaning of these sounds—seems to vary from area to area. Attack, flight and greeting behavior also vary.

These differences tend to be variations on common themes of behavior. Constant traits include the types of behavior used to strengthen bonds between individual baboons, particularly mutual grooming and the protection of offspring.

The behavioral variations in savannah baboons are principally a response to an unpredictable and difficult environment. They reflect, in their diversity, the potential of the higher primates to react to environmental changes—a potential which has been fulfilled most dramatically in humankind.

RIGHT TOP From time to time, male baboons may move to the head of a migrating procession to decide on the route or to confront predators.

RIGHT BOTTOM When searching for food or water, the members of a baboon troop spread out more than when they are on the march.

ABOVE After their first feed in the morning, baboons normally spend time grooming one another, choosing a place that offers a swift exit in case of danger. While grooming is going on, some members of the troop remain on the lookout for predators. The young are particularly vulnerable to leopards.

Bonnets and toques

Two monkeys of unusual appearance are the bonnet macaque and toque macaque. The bonnet macaque of southern India has a high forehead and a neat hairstyle with a central parting. The toque macaque of Sri Lanka has a more unruly mop that grows from lower down on the forehead and is the same shape as a beret.

Holy crab eaters

The crab-eating macaque is found in Java, many other Indonesian islands, the Philippines, the Malay Peninsula, most of Burma, and southern Southeast Asia. An agile animal with a long tail, it inhabits tropical forests near water, including coastal forests and mangrove swamps. Given this preference for water, it is not surprising that crab-eating macaques include aquatic animals such as crabs, shellfish and amphibians in their diet. The crab eaters are skilled swimmers and are able to capture prey underwater.

They are also considered sacred animals and are especially revered and protected on the island of Bali in Indonesia, where people traditionally leave them offerings of rice, fruit and other food at the entrances to their Hindu temples.

The Moor macaque inhabits the island of Sulawesi in Indonesia, where three subspecies have evolved on the three southern peninsulas. The other exclusively Sulawesian macaque is the Celebes macaque of the northern peninsula of Sulawesi. The male is about 25 in. long with pronounced cheekbones and a stiff tuft of hair on his head.

The baboons

These familiar Old World monkeys are generally larger than macaques. The largest baboon of all—the mandrill—is also the largest of all monkeys. It grows to about 35 in. long (including a tail that measures just 3 to 4 in. long), stands up to 24 in. tall at the shoulders and weighs as much as 110 lbs. when fully mature. Hamadryas baboons tend to be the smallest of the baboons; though they are only a little shorter than the mandrill, they are more slender and the males weigh up to about 37 lbs.

The mandrill and drill have hardly any tails, in contrast to the other baboons that have long tails—up to 24 in. in the savannah baboon—often carried with the first part horizontal and the last two-thirds vertical. In all the baboons, the female is much smaller than the male, sometimes reaching only half the latter's weight. The male often has a ruff around its neck and mane, particularly in large, old individuals.

Baboons have sturdy, dog-like heads, and long snouts with the nostrils at the tip. The ears are small, as are the eyes, which appear sunken because of the protruding brow. Like some other Old World monkeys and apes, baboons have patches of hard skin on their buttocks. These are known as ischial callosities (from "ischium," a bone in the pelvic girdle), and they make it more comfortable for the animal to sit on hard or rough surfaces. In the baboon, these callosities are naked and pronounced, especially in the males.

The baboon's body is thick-set, the limbs powerful and the shoulders higher than the rump. The body structure is well suited to life on the ground, but baboons are quite capable of climbing into the trees, which they do at night and as a last resort in escaping from marauding predators.

In female baboons the skin between the genital organs and anus (the perineal area) swells and colors during the first half of the menstrual cycle and goes down again after ovulation. The swelling acts as a clear visual signal to the males that the female is ready to mate; males will not try to mate with females that do not have a swelling. This signal, with its precise social significance, can also be observed in the apes.

A baboon's teeth have a most fearsome appearance. The canines are tusk-like, and all the other teeth are powerful. They are adapted to eating a wide variety of foods including roots, shoots, fruit and leaves, birds' eggs, and insects. Baboons do not chase and hunt animal prey, as they are not built for fast running, but they do eat a certain amount of meat. By searching carefully in grass for animals that freeze rather than flee, they can catch a newborn gazelle or young hare. When feeding, the animal stands on three limbs while collecting food and feeding with the hand of the fourth limb. It is adept at handling food since both the thumbs and the big toes are set some way apart from the other digits.

Baboons have a well-developed social organization. They live in large groups or troops of a dozen to a couple of hundred individuals, though the most usual number is about 50. Within these large groups there is a constant interplay between the different individuals, and the pattern of relationships changes all the time.

ABOVE While grooming each other, savannah baboons produce non-aggressive lip-smacking sounds. Baboons have a wide range of other calls, including barks, grunts, snores, buzzes, screams and chattering noises. All are important social signals, communicating changes of mood and passing information from one individual to another.

Troop commanders

Experienced mature males stand at the top of the troop's hierarchy and there are several of them within a troop. They control the troop, decide on its moving and feeding activities and protect the females and juveniles against any threats. When a troop of baboons is on the move, the dominant males keep to the center of the group together with females in heat and those with young, while immature males lead the way.

Dominant males retain their position at the top of the hierarchy until they are challenged and usurped by younger males that may even form alliances to confront the established males.

Conflicts are sometimes resolved by fighting, but more often, as is so often the case with animals, they take the form of ritualized behavior involving little or no physical contact. Baboons have one particularly fearsome display—the yawn, in which the long canines are exposed to their full extent and the eyebrows are drawn up so that they glare white at the rival.

The majority of baboon interaction is friendly, not hostile. When at rest, or after feeding, baboons gather for mutual grooming. The dominant males are often the center of attention, sought out by both the females and the young alike.

Pleasures of grooming

Grooming among baboons is partly carried out to remove parasites, to clean and condition the fur, and to scratch the skin, and partly to relax the animals. Physical contact of this kind has a social function unrelated to sexual intention. Humans, too, derive pleasure from non-sexual physical contact such as slapping a friend on the back in encouragement or putting arms around a child to comfort it. Stroking cats and dogs has been proved to reduce stress in humans, especially those who have little human contact.

ABOVE With his long cheek whiskers, silvery-gray shoulder ruff and larger size, a dominant male hamadryas baboon (to the right of the picture) is easily recognizable among the smaller, drabber females and juveniles in the harem.
BELOW Backed up by the menacing presence of a mature male baboon (right), a juvenile male (center) threatens another juvenile.

The bond that links young baboons to their mothers is a very close and physical one. Grooming in adults may be partly a ritual form of behavior developed from the relationship established between the mother and her newborn offspring.

Drinking companions

The various parts of each troop's home range are exploited at different times of the year, ensuring that sufficient food will be available all year round. The baboons thus avoid the need to venture into the territories of other groups. However, in the savannah, where there is a severe seasonal problem in finding enough water, several troops will share the same waterhole without fights or rivalry. At these times, the young baboons show a natural interest and curiosity in the younger members of other troops.

BABOONS CLASSIFICATION

True baboons of the genus *Papio* are confined to Africa south of the Sahara and to a restricted area of southern Arabia. The classification of baboons is complex, and different authorities have grouped them into different numbers of species. The baboons that live in open country include the savannah, hamadryas, western, and chacma baboons. The savannah baboon, *P. cynocephalus*, occurs over most of sub-Saharan Africa and varies from yellow to gray in color over the different parts of its range. The hamadryas baboon, *P. hamadryas*, occupies the eastern edges of the African continent in Ethiopia and Somalia and is also found in Saudi Arabia and South Yemen. The western baboon, *P. papio*, occurs in West Africa from Senegal south to Sierra Leone; and the chacma baboon, *P. ursinus*, ranges over southern Africa. The remaining members of the genus are inhabitants of the rain forests of southern Nigeria, Cameroon, Gabon, and Congo. The two species are classified in their own subgenus *Mandrillus*—the drill, *M. leucophaeus*, and the mandrill, *M. sphinx*.

One other monkey is commonly known as a baboon, though it belongs to a separate genus—the gelada or gelada baboon, *Theropithecus gelada*. It lives in thinly vegetated upland habitats, including mountain gorges, within the Ethiopian highlands.

Baboon relationships

It was long believed that baboons formed troops purely to make mating and breeding easier. It is now clear that this is far from the truth and that the social groupings provide all kinds of advantages to the animals. The lifelong relationships established by the females with their young, with the other females and with the males form the basis of the unity of the groups. Females spend their whole lives with the troop into which they are born. Males tend to move off into another group when they are in their early maturity, preventing inbreeding within the same family.

Sexually mature females are fertile for about one week in each month. During this time, they leave their customary companions and weaned offspring (though these still follow at a distance) and go off in search of males with which to mate. Each female first mates with adult males of relatively low rank or males that have recently reached maturity. Only when she is at her most fertile does she seek out high-ranking males. Fights may break out among the males for possession of the female, stimulated by her production of pheromones (chemical substances that are used to communicate with others of the species). The female may remain with the successful suitor for a few days.

The two animals usually stay around the edge of the group during the period of association and mating. After mating and ovulation, the pair-bond breaks down and the group re-forms as before. The social life of savannah baboons involves a large degree of promiscuity (indiscriminate sexual relations) with no harems or family units. At the same time, the baboons do also develop some close and long-lasting bonds with a few select individuals.

The hamadryas baboons

Mature hamadryas baboons are among the most magnificent of the primates in appearance. As they grow older the males develop a silver-gray ruff, which makes the animals stand out clearly among the duller brown juveniles and smaller females. These baboons live in arid areas, often on hilly, rock-covered outcrops—sometimes even in semidesert—and they feed on grass seeds and underground plant material such as bulbs, tubers, and roots that they dig up from the ground.

Hamadryas baboons were the sacred baboons of ancient Egypt, featured in art and religion and associated with Thoth, the god of learning. Many of their mummified bodies have been unearthed during excavations. Ironically, hamadryas baboons have been exterminated in modern-day Egypt.

Like the savannah baboons, hamadryas baboons form large troops that tend to sleep in the same area (on cliff faces in the case of the hamadryas). In both species, these troops divide into bands for daily foraging. But unlike the savannah baboons, the hamadryas bands divide further into clans of about 15-20 baboons, formed of one, two or three families.

Each family has one dominant male that has a harem of females and their attendant young. Young males are tolerated by the dominant male until they begin to show too much interest in the mature females. Then they may be driven out of the group, unless they are strong enough to usurp the harem owner and mate with some or all of his females.

Hamadryas society is united by the males rather than the females, since males tend to stay in and retain their harem, while the females move between families or clans. An immature female can be seduced by a male outside her family since the dominant male in her group will not strongly defend a female below breeding age. Another male can, therefore, associate with an immature female so that he will have a mate when she reaches maturity. Females may also change bands if they are kidnapped, or if young challengers defeat an aging ruler and take over his harem.

The movement of females is important in reducing or preventing interbreeding, since it mixes up the members of different families. It is also difficult for a young male to kidnap two females in succession from the same group, and his harem is therefore made up of females that are taken from a variety of genetically independent populations.

ABOVE Adult baboons often gather around a mother and her young one, lending protective support to the vulnerable offspring and maintaining the close social bonds within the troop. BELOW Within a clan of hamadryas baboons, each harem moves around with the male at the front and the females and young following (A). When two harems travel together, one male baboon stays at the head of the procession and one walks at the rear to fight off attacks by predators or intruding males (B).

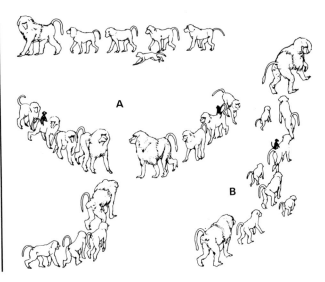

Leaping to the defense

Savannah baboon and hamadryas baboon behavior is similar when it comes to the defense of offspring or females. The animals display a strong degree of unity against an enemy, and several hamadryas groups will often combine to present a united front if they are threatened. The main enemies of savannah and hamadryas baboons are humans and the big cats, particularly the leopard. However, even though a leopard is capable of taking young baboons, it will rarely manage to outwit an adult baboon.

One account published in an African newspaper told of a fight between a leopard and a male baboon that ended in the death of both contenders, the baboon with its back broken against a tree and the leopard completely disemboweled.

In savannah areas, the baboons have to beware not only of predators, but of such nighttime dangers as poisonous scorpions and snakes. For safety, the baboons prefer to spend the night in the branches of one of the high trees scattered across the savannah.

Standing united

An example of group defense was recorded in the Tsavo National Park in eastern Kenya. A group of baboons were grazing peacefully among the tall savannah grasses when they were approached by several elephants coming to drink at a nearby river. The baboons ran to take refuge in a few tall palm trees, but there was not enough space to take the whole group. Amid excited shrieks, the larger, dominant baboons tried to take the best places for themselves and pushed the younger animals aside.

In the scramble, one of the young baboons fell to the ground only a few dozen yards from the advancing elephants. He stayed where he was, uttering cries of alarm and terror, since he had no means of escape or refuge. At this point, the whole group came down from the palm tree to aid their companion. They arranged themselves in a ring around the fallen baboon with the females and young animals at the center, while the larger males uttered vocal threats and bared their teeth angrily.

The huge commotion made by the baboons finally caused the elephants to turn aside to drink further downstream. Once the danger (probably more imagined than real) had passed, the baboons resumed their activities with apparent unconcern.

ABOVE The mandrill's brightly colored face consists of vivid patches of bare skin. The colors intensify when the animal is annoyed or excited. Perhaps because the mandrill's aggression is clearly indicated by color, the baring of teeth has lost the intimidatory significance it has among the baboons. Instead, when combined with side-to-side movements of the head, tooth baring has become an act of appeasement between individuals, and perhaps even a sign of friendship.

Drills and mandrills

Drills and mandrills are forest-dwelling baboons. The males are much larger than the females. Both have large heads with long snouts. The face is hairless and has deep ridges that are bright blue in the adult male mandrill. The mature male mandrill's nose and lips are bright scarlet; the mask-like effect of the features is striking. During threat displays, the pattern gives the animal an intimidating appearance.

Mandrills and drills prefer to stay on the ground where they search for their mainly vegetarian food, but they climb trees to search for fruit, to flee from danger and to sleep. Although their diet is mainly vegetarian, they will also take animal foods and indeed often capture insects, worms and small vertebrates. Groups vary from a few individuals to as many as 60, and they tend to stay within a fairly well-defined home range.

ABOVE Though geladas are more mild-mannered than baboons, they take on a fierce appearance when they are annoyed. At such times geladas draw back their lips to expose their long canines and they lower their white eyelids. Geladas also have patches of bare skin on their necks and chests that flush bright red when they are excited.

Drills and mandrills probably have a hamadryas-like social structure, with small harems led by a single large mature male; the harems sometimes unite to form larger groups. They are very vocal animals, barking, grunting, roaring and shrieking to keep in touch, since they cannot always see each other among the foliage of the trees.

Bright hues

The males have brightly colored, naked rears of pink, violet and red. These colors, along with the face coloration, make drills and mandrills unmistakable. The function of the brightly colored hindquarters is unknown, but may perhaps act as a visual signal in the gloom of the forests. It may also be used to establish individual rank without bloodshed. When a mandrill or drill is threatened by a rival or feels frightened, it presents its rear—a variation on a typical female monkey's demonstration of sexual receptiveness. This may act as a signal that the threatened animal's intentions are not aggressive.

In drill and mandrill society, older males are responsible for defense. When they feel threatened, these animals not only bare their teeth and show off their striking coloration, but they also stretch out their arms and plant their feet firmly on the ground in a defensive posture, ready to face their enemy.

In captivity, drills and mandrills have a reputation for being unpredictable. It should be remembered, however, that these animals are often kept on their own in zoos. Deprived of a social relationship with other animals, their behavior patterns alter and they can easily become aggressive. Like baboons, mandrills and drills need the social interaction of activities such as grooming in order to maintain the stability that is commonly found in groups in the wild.

The gelada

The gelada baboon has thick fur, strong nails, and a heavily built body that make it ideally adapted for life in its inhospitable habitat—the almost bare, rocky terrain of the Ethiopian highlands.

The gelada baboon differs from the "true" baboons in having a much higher voice and a quite different head shape: rounded, with upturned nostrils. It feeds almost entirely on vegetable matter, also taking the occasional insect. Its distribution follows the lines of major escarpments, or cliffs. The animals sleep on the cliff faces, leaving them to feed during the day, returning to them at night or when in any danger.

Despite their imposing appearance, gelada baboons are actually mild-mannered, only showing aggression in defense of their harems. When an enemy threatens the group, the baboons quickly and fearlessly drive it away by throwing stones and other heavy objects at it. Many Abyssinian legends recount the deeds of this monkey that is supposed to form bands to catch unwary travelers. Small numbers of geladas are kept—and they regularly breed—in zoos.

Mangabeys

The mangabeys are closely related to the baboons and occur in forested land over much of equatorial Africa. The four species fall into two groups that differ in their habits. The agile and white mangabeys are both predominantly terrestrial monkeys that move about on all fours over the forest floor. The gray-

cheeked and black mangabeys, on the other hand, are almost entirely arboreal or tree-dwelling.

The mangabeys weigh up to 22 lbs. and measure up to about 28 in. in length, excluding their long tails. The males are a little larger than the females, but otherwise the sexes look similar. Coat color varies considerably from species to species, ranging from gray to brown or black. In the white mangabey, the hair on the neck and along the back forms a dark stripe, while the agile mangabey's hair forms a high crest on its head.

Nutcrackers

Although it is not fully prehensile, the managbey's tail is used for support; the gray-cheeked mangabey uses its tail to improve its grip on branches. The monkeys all have elongated faces, prominent brows, and cheek pouches in which they store food. They have strong incisors suitable for eating hard nuts. The guenons, with which the mangabeys share many habitats, do not have this ability and so do not compete for this source of food.

Like many of the Old World monkeys, mangabeys have a considerable range of facial expressions. They are also highly vocal monkeys, and the gray-cheeked mangabey's "whoop-gobble" call is a familiar sound in

ABOVE LEFT White mangabeys have folds of brilliant white skin over their eyes that make eyelid and brow movements more visible. These movements, along with those of the mouth and tongue, are the basis of communication between the monkeys. **ABOVE Gray-cheeked mangabeys rarely descend to ground level. They live in forests over many parts of Central Africa, preferring habitats close to rivers.**

the rain forests of Zaire in Central Africa. It serves to keep members of a troop together in the woods and to keep neighboring troops apart. Although they roam over an extensive area without establishing clear territories, the monkey troops remain separate, and if two troops meet they may clash fiercely. They are inquisitive animals and search for food continually, sometimes raiding cultivated fields, for which they are considered pests by farmers.

The colorful guenons

The 15 species of guenons may comprise as many as 70 subspecies distributed throughout Africa, making the classification of the group extremely difficult. Their coats—unlike those of the macaques and baboons—are colorful, with vivid tones and contrasts; guenons are the most variably colored of all the Old World monkeys.

Guenons' slender bodies measure 14-28 in. in length, and their tails are another 20-35 in. long. Their weight rarely exceeds 22 lbs., though the males are considerably larger than the females. The head of a guenon is rounded, the brow is not notably pronounced, and the snout is short. They have large cheek pouches, and young animals have a prehensile tail.

Guenons probably began to diverge into their many subspecies relatively recently in evolutionary terms. The great variety of color forms in the group can be bewildering and make it difficult to distinguish the different species, but there are usually one or two features that are peculiar to each.

Distinguishing features

The vervet is generally a light gray-green with variations in its coloration occurring across its geographical range. The blue monkey has white underparts, a dark ruff, and bristly hair on the forehead. The diana monkey—one of the most brightly colored guenons—has a gray body, tawny-red back, white markings on the inside of its limbs and a particularly striking white, triangular facial ruff. De Brazza's monkey has a black face, a brown brow and a short, white ruff; despite its wide distribution, it is perhaps the least variable species in terms of coat color.

RIGHT Guenons are sociable monkeys, living in small family groups dominated by a single male, but congregating in larger troops for feeding and resting. When they discover a particularly rich crop of fruit on a forest tree, or when they are raiding cultivated areas, they may gather in huge assemblies containing several hundred individuals.

The mona monkey has a flesh-colored muzzle contrasting with a blue face, and it has a crest on the crown of its head. The spot-nosed, redtail and lesser spot-nosed monkeys all have white patches on the nose, but their tails differ: the spot-nosed has a long black tail, the lesser spot-nosed's tail is brown and black above and white below, and the redtail, as its name suggests, has a mainly reddish tail. The mustached monkey has a white chevron on its upper lip, which the otherwise similar red-nosed monkey lacks. Hamlyn's monkey has a flattened, wrinkled face and enormous eyes—hence its alternative name, the owl-faced monkey.

Monkey of the savannah

The grassland-dwelling vervet is the most widely distributed of the guenons and one of the best-known African monkeys. It lives on savannah lands near thorn scrub and wooded areas, where it shelters

---

MANGABEYS AND GUENONS CLASSIFICATION

In addition to the macaques and baboons, there are five genera within the subfamily Cercopithicinae that are native only to Africa. The four species of mangabeys belong to the genus *Cercocebus*: the gray-cheeked mangabey, *C. albigena*, which ranges from Cameroon to Uganda; the white or collared mangabey, *C. torquatus*, of West and Central Africa; the black mangabey, *C. aterrimus*, of Zaire; and the agile or crested mangabey, *C. galeritus*, which has separate ranges in Central and East Africa.

The 15 or so species of guenons in the genus *Cercopithecus* are monkeys of savannah and forest habitats south of the Sahara. They include the vervet or green monkey, *Cercopithecus aethiops*, which occurs across most of sub-Saharan Africa; the blue or diadem monkey, *C. mitis*, of Central and East Africa; the diana monkey, *C. diana*, which occurs in West Africa from Sierra Leone to Ghana; De Brazza's monkey, *C. neglectus*, of Central Africa; the mona monkey, *C. mona*, found from Ghana to southwest Cameroon; the lesser spot-nosed monkey, *C. petuarista*, which has a similar range to the diana monkey; the mustached monkey, *C. cephus*, which ranges along the west coast of Central Africa from southern Cameroon to northern Angola; and the owl-faced or Hamlyn's monkey, *C. hamlyni*, of eastern Zaire and Rwanda.

The remaining three genera each comprise only one species. Allen's swamp monkey, *Allenopithecus nigroviridis*, lives in Congo and Zaire, while the talapoin monkey, *Miopithecus talapoin*, ranges from Cameroon south to Angola. The patas monkey, *Erythrocebus patas*, occurs in a belt of semi-arid and savannah land from Senegal east to Ethiopia and Tanzania.

Black mangabey

Lesser spot-nosed monkey

Patas monkey

Vervet

Diana monkey

De Brazza's monkey

during the night. It also keeps close to water and is often sighted on riverbanks. Vervets live in groups containing up to 50 animals, but averaging some 10-15. They feed out on the open land during the day, eating fruits, roots, bulbs, spiders, insects and sometimes lizards and young birds. Some individuals are solitary—these are probably old or unsociable monkeys that have adapted to life outside the community, refusing all contact and acting aggressively toward other vervets.

The other guenons are all arboreal species, and each is extremely well adapted to a specific type of habitat. One area of forest may accommodate several species, all keeping out of each other's way as they feed on slightly different foods at different levels in the trees. De Brazza's monkey lives in swamp forests, but the others all inhabit rain forests and upland tropical forests.

Though vervets tend to avoid thickly forested areas where species better adapted to such a habitat usually live, they are quick to move into such environments if there is no competition. The same pattern is found among other guenons—if one species is absent from a forest, others may invade its vacant slot among the forest habitats in order to increase their own living space.

The tiny talapoin

Three other monkeys are sometimes referred to as guenons, though they are classified separately from the species already described. The talapoin monkey is

ABOVE The diana monkey is an animal of the high forest canopy, living in groups of up to 50 males, females and young. Each troop occupies a territory covering about half a square mile at treetop level. During territorial disputes, the monkeys display by hanging from a branch with their hands between their feet, and presenting their contrastingly colored backsides to their challengers.

UNDER THREAT

THE GUENONS

The guenons face the pressure that burdens all the inhabitants of tropical forests—relentless destruction of their environment. L'Hoest's monkey is a case in point. Occurring in upland forests in two separate regions of Central Africa, it is declining rapidly in places where the forest has been reduced and fragmented, but it remains abundant in other areas. In the western section of its range, the population is in a critical state—only in protected reserves are the monkeys likely to find a safe refuge.

The diana monkey is similarly threatened by destruction of the forests, but other human actions compound its problems. It is hunted for its flesh in parts of West Africa, killed as an agricultural pest, though there is little evidence that it actually damages crops, and, owing to its colorful fur, it is taken from the wild as a popular pet. The effects on the population have long been recognized—the diana monkey was already rare in Liberia, the Ivory Coast and Ghana by the 1950s—but the decline in numbers continues.

Despite its wide distribution in Central, East and southern Africa, the blue monkey is also becoming increasingly rare. One of its subspecies, the golden monkey of eastern Zaire, numbers no more than a few hundred animals.

TOP The mona monkey is a guenon of West and Central Africa, noted for its speed in moving through forest branches. Habitat loss and hunting have taken their toll on most species of guenons in Africa, and several species are now endangered.

ABOVE A mustached monkey in an aggressive posture—males utter sharp calls when their territory is threatened by intruding monkeys. Like mona monkeys, they are agile creatures, able to leap across 65 ft. gaps between the trees.

the smallest Old World monkey. It is little bigger than a large squirrel—about 14 in. in length—with a tail up to 15 in. long and a maximum weight of 3 lbs. 5 oz. It lives in groups and inhabits the wettest forest areas. The talapoin feeds mainly on fruit, seeds, flowers and leaves and, like a squirrel, it is very agile.

Allen's swamp monkey is quite similar to the mangabeys and baboons; it was first recognized as a species not in the wild but in London Zoo in 1907. Little is known about its habits except that it occupies the same wet wooded habitat as the talapoin and De Brazza's monkey, and feeds on aquatic invertebrates as well as plants.

High-speed runner

The patas monkey is a slender, almost gaunt monkey that inhabits dry areas on savannah land and rocky plateaus. It is the largest of the guenons and the fastest of all the primates, with a running speed of over 30 mph. Although it occupies the same type of arid habitat as baboons, it lives in smaller groups and is both shy and quiet. Mainly vegetarian, it also eats invertebrates, small lizards and birds.

Patas field studies

Animals are often secretive and shy, and they can be difficult to study in their natural habitat. Even though people have been chasing animals for centuries—hunting them for food and sport, and more recently observing and filming them—a surprisingly small number have been recorded in any detail in the wild. Studies have concentrated on a few well-known species such as lions and elephants, though even these familiar beasts are by no means fully understood.

Among the primates, some animals have been extensively studied, while little is known of many others. Baboons have received much attention, partly because of the relative ease of observing open-country species. In the early 1960s the British scientist K.R.L. Hall carried out important work on baboon behavior in the wild. He also turned his attention to investigating the behavior of another open-country species—the patas monkey.

Hall spent over 650 hours of fieldwork observing a group of patas monkeys in the Kabalega Falls National Park (formerly Murchison Falls National Park) in Uganda. He found some interesting contrasts between the adaptations, ecology (the relationshp of the animal with its surroundings), and behavior of patas monkeys and baboons.

Patas monkeys are medium-sized, reaching about 5 ft. in length, about half of which is tail. The males may weigh over 22 lbs. and are much bigger than the females, which rarely exceed 15 lbs. The patas monkey is also known as the red guenon because of its russet upperparts. The males sometimes have a long, impressive mane. Unlike those of the baboons, the patas monkey's hind limbs are as long as its forelimbs, and the monkeys often stand upright to scan their surroundings.

Like the savannah baboon, however, the patas monkey is active during the day (diurnal) and is mainly terrestrial. It haunts savannah and lightly wooded land, keeping away from denser areas of forest.

A mixed diet

Hall found that patas monkeys formed groups of between nine and 31 individuals, the average being around 15. Each group occupied an extensive home range of greatly varying size, up to about 12,500 acres. Their diet contains a considerable amount of fruit—especially the seed-filled pods of the acacia, a tree that often dominates the dry, open, lightly wooded savannah. Apart from fruit, they take leaves, roots, tree gum, as well as occasional insects, small vertebrates and birds' eggs. The animals drink infrequently at waterholes.

Hall tracked various patas monkeys to establish how large an area they covered each day in search of food, and the distances covered by groups throughout the seasons. When food was scarce, the monkeys traveled much farther. The maximum distance covered in a day was 7.5 mi., whereas the minimum distance was not more than 1640 ft.

A midday nap

The daily routine included two main feeding periods, one in the morning and one in the evening, separated by a nap or rest lasting one to three hours at the hottest time of day. The groups tended to use different areas of their territory for resting at night, in contrast to baboons in the same area that had a "core zone" where they would habitually return to sleep. Each patas monkey chose a separate tree in which to sleep on their own, except for the nursing mothers that would keep their infants with them.

ABOVE The talapoin is the smallest of the Old World monkeys, weighing under three and a half pounds. Inhabiting Central Africa, it forages for fruit, leaves, and insects in swamp **forests and in the trees alongside rivers and streams. In many places it shares the riverbanks with humans that come to wash their clothes or to catch fish.**

A patas monkey group consists of one adult male, his female attendants and their young. The male tends to be something of a loner, often leaving the group to survey potential new feeding areas or to check for danger. Except for periods of rest, mating or grooming, he stays on the edge of the group.

The male group leader acts as guardian to his group. Every time the group is disturbed or moves to a new area, the male surveys the new territory from a high vantage point. Hall found that if the male was disturbed, he would jump up and down, making low calls, usually while standing in a bush or tree—perhaps to attract attention away from the rest of the group.

Within the group, it is the females that initiate activities and that are responsible for organizing marches. Adult females are also responsible for taking care of offspring and young animals. Although there is no elaborate courtship ritual, the female signals her readiness for mating with a low run toward the male,

As well as the male-led mixed groups, lone males were also observed, along with groups consisting only of males. The complete structure of patas monkey society is unknown; perhaps lone males or males from the all-male groups take over mixed groups when leaders die. Single males may join mixed troops during the mating season.

The patas monkey groups are so widely spaced that Hall seldom observed encounters between them. On the rare occasions that groups met, the larger group generally chased away the smaller one. The lack of contact between groups and the threat of predators in open country may well have been responsible for reducing the range of sounds the patas monkeys make, in clear contrast to baboons. In general, patas monkeys tend to make soft, low call sounds. Hall only once noted a male uttering a bark at meeting members of another group.

The contrasts between patas monkeys and baboons are marked. The former are lightly built and adapted to running fast on four limbs. The monkeys lead largely silent concealed lives in widely scattered social groups. The baboons, on the other hand, are notoriously noisy and form larger, more aggressive groups—probably because more than one male is present in every troop.

The long-tailed monkeys

The colobine monkeys form a different subfamily from the macaques, guenons and baboons; it covers the langurs and leaf, snub-nosed, douc and colobus monkeys. They lack cheek pouches and have complex stomachs and large salivary glands. Colobines are usually tree dwellers, and their tails are always long.

Colobine monkeys are vegetarian, and their bodies are adapted to eating large amounts of vegetable matter. The molar teeth are suitable for chewing leaves, and their stomachs—like those of ruminants—are divided into two chambers that can hold up to three times the contents of the average monkey's stomach. Acid in the lower stomach allows normal digestive procedures to take place. Bacteria in the upper stomach break down the tough leaves and neutralize poison found in some of the plants and fruit the monkeys eat.

Colobines tend to be less lively than other monkeys because of the difficulties they have in digesting their food. They spend a lot of time just sitting around in the

ABOVE When a patas monkey is alarmed it raises its eyebrows and drops its lower jaw in an expression of fear. Facial gestures are the main form of communication within patas troops. Since the animals normally live in areas of sparse vegetation, these visual signals are not obscured by leaves. Unless they are alarmed, they rarely use contact calls, and the few sounds they do utter when moving through the trees are usually low in volume so as not to attract predators.

the tip of her tail curved back, her lips pursed and cheeks puffed out. Females first become pregnant at about two and a half years old.

Hall observed that babies and young animals often played together for long periods, chasing each other and indulging in mock fights, games that equip the young for the activities of maturity.

Grooming activity among patas monkeys is intense and similar to that of baboons. Submission was rare in their social interaction. Presentation of the rear and symbolic mounting—when an individual monkey shows its superiority over one of its fellows through mock mating—were never observed. These forms of behavior are frequent in baboons and other monkeys, and used to be interpreted as an expression of homosexuality when observed among males. In fact they have no connection with true sexual activity.

RIGHT Hanuman langurs are the sacred monkeys of India and the descendants or representatives, according to Indian religion, of the monkey god Hanuman. For this reason, they are allowed to wander freely through towns where they are fed and revered.
BOTTOM On the ground, the hanuman langur is a strong leaper, able to jump easily across narrow streams and canals.

trees. Since leaves are fibrous and low in nutritional value, the monkeys need a long digestive process in order to extract the maximum nourishment from them. Colobus monkeys prefer not to move around too much while their stomachs are full, preferring to find a quiet spot where they can sit and digest their meal. As a result, their tranquil behavior makes the monkeys look as if they are meditating or praying, and this may partly explain why the animal is so revered in much of southern Asia.

Langurs and leaf monkeys

The hanuman langur is an adaptable and successful animal living in hills and valleys among scrub, forest and open woodland from sea level to over 13,000 ft. Males and females vary considerably in size with adult males weighing up to 44 lbs., whereas females average 25 lbs. Males are more than twice the size of females and reach a length of 70 in.; as much as 3 ft. of this may consist of tail. Hanumans vary greatly in appearance, and have been divided into as many as 15 subspecies.

Golden snub-nosed monkey

Western red colobus

Hanuman langur

Guereza

Proboscis monkey

Red-shanked douc

Purple-faced leaf monkey

The hanuman langur has a slender body and hands and a small thumb. In general, the upperparts of the coat are gray or gray-brown tinged with yellow; the crown, underparts and tail tip are white and the paws are brown or black. The hanuman is the sacred monkey of India, revered by Hindus and referred to in Indian folk tradition and in sacred texts.

John's langur is another slender and relatively agile colobine occupying wet evergreen forests. On Cat Ba Island in Vietnam, it lives in the gnarled and stunted woods of the poor limestone soils of the hills.

The leaf monkeys, like a number of the colobines, have fine fur that grows like a cap on the head. The silvered leaf monkey, a sociable creature found in villages of Southeast Asia as well as in forest and scrub, has an attractive little crest on the top of its

—— THE LEAF MONKEYS ——

UNDER THREAT

Many species of colobine monkeys are considered under threat, and several leaf monkeys are among those regarded as the most vulnerable. As forest dwellers, the chief problem they face, once again, is habitat destruction. The dusky leaf monkey has declined rapidly in Malaysia, and though it remains common in parts of Thailand the tide of deforestation threatens to overwhelm the population even there. The silvered leaf monkey has also suffered greatly in Malaysia—its numbers were reduced by a third from 1958 to 1975 and the decline is almost certain to have continued since then. The scarce Phayre's leaf monkey has had to contend with additional pressures. In Burma large numbers of these primates were once hunted for their gallstones, which were used in traditional medicine.

ABOVE Like all colobines, the spectacled or dusky leaf monkey of the Malay Peninsula eats tree foliage as the main part of its diet, preferring tender young leaves and consuming up to 4 lbs. 4 oz. every day. It also eats flowers, buds and fruit.

ABOVE LEFT When faced with danger, the langur (A) usually takes refuge in a tree, whereas the macaque (B) may assume a defensive posture without, or before, running away. Leopards and smaller cats are the main predators of langurs and macaques.

LEFT The silvered leaf monkey owes its name to the white or yellowish tips of its body hair that give its long, soft fur a silvery appearance.

BELOW LEFT As a young langur grows into an adult, it gradually changes its repertoire of calls (top), and develops new gestures and attitudes (bottom).

head; the dusky leaf monkey, in the northern parts of its range, has a crest.

Several langurs, including John's langur, have been persecuted for their coats, which are soft and often colorful. Langurs have also been hunted for their meat, which is held in high regard for its flavor and for its supposed medicinal qualities. The intestines of leaf monkeys often contain chalky deposits known as bezoars (they are also found in certain ruminants, such as goats and ibexes). Bezoars are believed to have special healing powers and are much sought after and highly prized in traditional Chinese medicine. Like rhino horn—another animal product sought for its supposed healing powers—the hunting of leaf monkeys for bezoar is now threatening their survival.

LANGURS AND LEAF MONKEYS CLASSIFICATION

Some 20 species within the subfamily Colobinae are grouped into the genus Presbytis—the langurs and leaf monkeys. Mostly forest dwellers, they range from India through Southeast Asia to Indonesia. The hanuman, entellus or common langur, *Presbytis entellus*, is the sacred langur of the Indian subcontinent, ranging from the Himalayas southward to Sri Lanka. The John's or Nilgiri langur, *P. johnii*, lives in southern India and on Cat Ba Island in Vietnam. The silvered leaf monkey, *P. cristatus*, is widespread in Southeast Asia, while the dusky or spectacled leaf monkey, *P. obscurus*, occupies the Malay Peninsula and nearby islands. The capped or bonneted leaf monkey, *P. pileatus*, is found in Bangladesh, Burma and Assam; and the purple-faced leaf monkey, *S. vetulus*, in Sri Lanka. Five species of langurs are sometimes grouped together as the surelis, including the mitered langur or black-crested sureli, *Presbytis melalophos*, of southwest Sumatra; and the Mentawai Islands langur or red-bellied sureli, *P. potenziani*, of the Mentawai Islands in Indonesia.

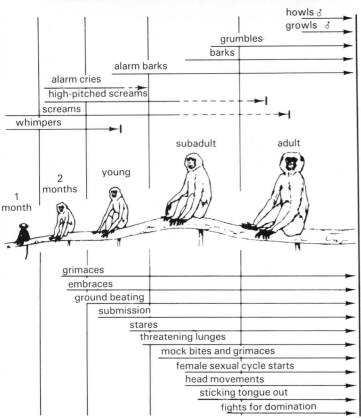

Doucs and snub-nosed monkeys

The douc langurs and the snub-nosed monkeys (like the proboscis and pig-tailed snub-nosed monkeys) have arms and legs of about the same length; in the rest of the colobine group the arms of the monkeys are considerably shorter than the legs.

The doucs are among the most striking of all the monkeys, patterned in chestnut, black and white. Once common in Vietnam, they have become extremely rare, decimated by hunting and the ravages of the Vietnam War.

The snub-nosed monkeys are sturdily built and have upturned noses and nostrils. In contrast, the doucs have flatter noses. The snub-nosed monkeys inhabit mountain areas and have long, thick coats. They are 4-5 ft. in length, about half of which is tail; doucs are approximately the same size.

Snub-nosed monkeys are seen only rarely in the wild since they are retiring by nature and inhabit inaccessible areas. However, they are known to travel in large bands and to eat fruit, leaves and bamboo shoots. The golden snub-nosed monkey reaches so high in the mountains of south and central China that it must migrate to lower elevations in winter to avoid heavy snow.

The rarest snub-nosed monkey is the Brelich's or Guizhou golden monkey. A remnant population of perhaps 500 animals is found at Fanjing Mountain reserve, where they live in four or five groups, ranging from as few as 20 to as many as 200 individuals.

All the Chinese snub-nosed monkeys are rare and threatened. All have been hunted for their coats and for meat. Fortunately, they have received increasing protection, and it may not be too late to save them.

Two odd primates

The proboscis monkey must be one of the most unusual looking primates. A bulky animal (males measure up to 30 in. long with the same length of tail and weigh over 44 lbs.), it owes its name to the male's huge nose (or "proboscis," meaning "trunk" in Greek),

ABOVE RIGHT With its black and white coat, deep red legs and bare, orange face, the red-shanked douc is one of the most distinctively colored of all the monkeys. It inhabits the rain forests and monsoon forests of Laos and Vietnam.
RIGHT Little is known of the behavior of red-shanked doucs; they are rare, difficult to observe in the wild and troublesome to rear in captivity.

THE HANUMAN LANGUR
— INDIA'S SACRED MONKEY —

Of all the primates, one species in particular has had a much longer link with human affairs than any other, playing a role in the history, religion and culture of an entire country: the hanuman langur of India.

The monkey gets it name from Hanuman, the monkey god of the Hindu religion who was able to fly and change his shape. In the Ramayana (the Romance of Rama), an epic poem of India written some two thousand years ago, Hanuman helps the supreme god Vishnu rescue Vishnu's wife after she has been kidnapped and taken to the island of Sri Lanka. There is also a fable about how Hanuman got his black paws. It is said that Hanuman had found and stolen the mango fruit while he was in Sri Lanka, bringing it back to India. For this theft, Hanuman was punished by being set on fire. As he put out the fire he singed his paws, which have remained forever black.

From forest to savannah

The Hanuman langur is probably the most abundant primate of the Indian subcontinent—after the humans. There are about one million of the monkeys, ranging from the slopes of the Himalayas in the north to Sri Lanka in the south, and from the Indus in Pakistan, across northern India to the Ganges Delta in Bangladesh. It is able to thrive in open as well as wooded habitats and lives on the ground when trees are sparse. An adaptable creature, the hanuman can survive environments that vary from extremely arid savannah with sparse, bushy vegetation to the most luxuriant, tropical forests.

The behavior of hanuman langurs varies strikingly according to the region that they inhabit.

Population densities in the hanuman are lowest in open grassland and in some farmed environments, where there may be less than five monkeys per half a square mile; in forests there may be more than 100 monkeys per half a square mile. Their diet comprises mainly leaves, but also includes fruit, flowers, berries and grain.

The female hanuman starts to breed at the age of three and a half years. The gestation period lasts for six months, and the mother suckles her single offspring for up to one year. Births therefore take place about every two years. Some infants—depending on the region in which they live—have been observed to suckle for up to two years. Sometimes, an older offspring and a newly born hanuman have been seen to suckle at the same time, from the same mother. The offspring leaves its mother when it is six months old; when it is nine months old and regarded as a subadult, the dominant male expels it from the group. New-born hanumans are colored dark brown and remain so for three to five months, after which they begin to turn the color of the adult: silvery-haired body, with black hands, soles of the feet, ears and face. Their face, with its black, bristly eyebrows, is encircled by a fringe of whitish fur. Although mothers are protective of their young, they allow the females in the troop to gather round

and touch, lick and hold the infant soon after it is born.

Unthreatened

Visitors to India soon discover how inquisitive and intrusive these sacred monkeys can be (although macaques are even worse offenders), for hanumans live close to humans in towns and villages, and especially in temples where they are allowed to roam about at will. Hindus regard them as sacred and often feed them, especially on Tuesday, which is regarded as Hanuman's day. Buddhists are no threat either since they do not believe in causing harm to any living thing.

Crop raiding

The hanuman langurs, however, like to eat crop plants and in heavily cultivated areas they have driven some farmers to the limits of their patience. The hanumans may even become dependent on crop raiding for their supplies of food. They also take food from merchants' stores in villages. There are stories of people who have exported their local hanumans by trains bound for some distant location. Some hunt the hanuman for its meat. Where it is in decline, this is due to destruction of its habitat.

LEFT Hanuman langurs rest during the midday heat, concentrating on their feeding activities in the cooler daylight hours of the early morning and late afternoon. These are the most terrestrial of the langurs, spending from 50 to 80 percent of their day on the ground.
ABOVE RIGHT Hanuman langurs are adaptable enough to thrive both in open land and woodland, and can even tolerate arid areas with minimal supplies of water.
RIGHT Although neighboring troops of hanumans frequently confront each other in disputes over territorial boundaries, they intermingle freely in certain circumstances, especially when drinking at waterholes.

The colobine monkeys live in southern and Southeast Asia and in equatorial Africa.

which can measure up to 4 in. in length. The nose is also evident in females and, although smaller than that of the male, is still larger than the nose of any other monkey. Young animals have upturned noses, whereas adult males have drooping noses that reach down to their mouths. To eat, adult males must actually move the nose to one side.

Zoologists have long tried to understand the function of this huge nose, and it has been suggested that it is used to boost the volume of the voice and to add a particular nasal quality. In the mangrove swamps of Borneo where it lives, the proboscis monkey is an excellent swimmer, feeding on aquatic vegetation. Its diet consists almost entirely of leaves, though it also takes some flowers and fruit. The proboscis is a sociable monkey; troops may vary in number from 10 to as many as 60 animals.

The pig-tailed snub-nosed monkey is in the same genus as the proboscis monkey, but differs from it in having a smaller nose rather similar to that of the snub-nosed monkey. Its tail is also short—just 6 in. long. These features make the pig-tailed snub-nosed monkey superficially resemble the pig-tailed macaque more than the monkeys in its own family. It is found in high forest, feeding on leaves and fruit, and it hardly ever descends to the ground.

Colobus monkeys

Although most of the modern colobines are Asian, the colobus monkeys are African. Even so, they probably evolved in Asia. Only during the late Tertiary period (about 10 million years ago) did early colobines reach the African continent, where they evolved independently to produce two modern-day genera. These are subdivided into seven species, one of which—the red colobus—has numerous subspecies.

African colobus monkeys are medium-sized monkeys. Their head and body length varies from as little as 17 in. in the olive colobus to over 27 in. in the black colobus and guereza. The tail is always long,

ABOVE LEFT **The extraordinary inflated nose of the proboscis monkey is considerably smaller in females and offspring than it is in males. The development of the nose appears to be closely** linked to the type of calls uttered by the male. LEFT **The jumping action of a proboscis monkey as it descends from a high branch on one forest tree to a branch lower down on another.**

ABOVE Guerezas make acrobatic leaps between trees, sometimes using the natural springiness of supple branches to catapult themselves into the air. When her young are clinging to her side or her chest, a female guereza takes shorter leaps, holding onto the young firmly with one hand.
PAGES 832-833 Guerezas spend nearly all their life in the forest canopy; they may move into the lower branches to escape from large birds of prey, but they rarely descend as far as ground level.

reaching up to 36 inches in the black colobuses and over 30 inches in the reds. Weights in the group range from 6 pounds in the olive colobus to more than 30 pounds in the guereza.

The black colobuses differ from the reds in several respects, most obviously in coat coloration but also in the number of chambers into which their stomachs are divided: three chambers in the black colobus and four in the red.

In the colobus monkeys, like in the New World spider monkeys, the thumb is stumpy. The name "colobus" was first given to the guerezas, and is derived from the Greek *kolobus*, meaning mutilated or maimed—a reference to the short thumb. It was thought that the thumbs of the first few specimens examined by scientists had been cut off.

— DOUCS AND SNUB-NOSED — MONKEYS CLASSIFICATION

Several species of colobine monkeys from mainland East Asia belong to the genus *Pygathrix*. The two douc monkeys—the red-shanked douc, *P. nemaeus*, and the very closely related black-shanked douc, *P. nigripes*—occur in Vietnam, Laos and Kampuchea and have often been classified as a single species. The red-shanked douc occupies the northern part of the pair's range and the black-shanked the southern. The other members of the genus are known as snub-nosed monkeys. They include the golden or orange snub-nosed monkey, *P. roxellana*, and Brelich's snub-nosed monkey, *P. brelichi*, both of which inhabit evergreen forests in mountainous regions of China.

The genus *Nasalis* also includes a snub-nosed species—the pig-tailed snub-nosed monkey, *N. concolor*, of the Mentawai Islands west of Sumatra. The only other member of the genus is the proboscis monkey, *N. larvatus*, which also occurs in Indonesia, inhabiting the mangrove and lowland rain forests of Borneo.

ABOVE The guereza is declining in many parts of its range, not only because of habitat destruction but also because it is widely hunted for its attractive fur. Millions of skins were exported from Africa in the late 19th century, many for use as rugs.

RIGHT The Angolan black and white colobus has a completely black back, in contrast to the guereza's tufty white mantle. It is found in parts of Central and East Africa. Though mainly a forest species, it frequently occurs in areas of maize cultivation.

The colobus monkeys have long, striking coats. Except for the black colobus, which is entirely black, the rest of the black colobus monkey group is patterned black and white; the coats of red colobuses bear reddish colors—often including bright oranges—with black and white markings. The olive colobus is an exception. Its olive-green coat is suffused with red.

Young colobus monkeys are born completely white and spend the first week of life in their mother's arms, after which they cling onto her coat. The female olive colobus, alone among African monkeys, carries her offspring in her mouth for the first few days.

Several of the colobuses are becoming quite rare; they were at one time hunted for their fur, and although a much greater degree of protection is now afforded them, there is still loss of their forest habitat through logging and clearance.

Langurs and macaques

The basis of our information on hanuman langurs comes from the work of the American scholar Phyllis Jay Dolhinow. Dolhinow studied the social life of several bands of hanuman langurs in northern India from 1958 to 1960. Her work and that of later field naturalists and behaviorists have given us a detailed picture of the daily habits and social organization of these abundant and adaptable primates.

The daily routine and degree of interaction of hanuman langur groups are in marked contrast to those of, say, a macaque group. The contrast is especially noticeable because hanuman langurs are found living alongside macaques throughout northern India. The two different species often live in the same area and even exploit the same food resources. They sleep in the same trees and drink from the same waterholes.

Macaques never seem to stay still. They are quickly aroused to threat displays and are more aggressive and much noisier than hanuman langurs. The hanumans, like all the colobines, show much less enthusiasm for social interaction. One reason for this may be the respective feeding habits of the two primates. The macaque has a mixed diet and will spend a great deal of time in food hunting, disputes and group movements. By contrast, a hanuman, as a leaf and fruit eater, often stays in one tree for a large part of the day, keeping to itself while it rests and digests its food.

Hanuman langurs do not protect the individual through group action as do the macaques and the baboons, and groups do not depend upon the protection given by large and aggressive adult males. When threatened, each hanuman langur retreats to the nearest tree.

Hanuman troops

Hanuman langurs live in troops, which vary in size and in sexual composition according to the environment. In areas where the monkeys are widely spaced, troops may contain over 100 animals and consist of males and females. Such large troops may be aggregations of smaller groups.

In areas where the monkey populations are denser and where there is more competition for resources, the troops tend to be smaller and to be composed of a single male with his harem of females. Such groups are territorial and have a clearly defined, permanent home range. There are also individual males and nomadic, all-male troops. When groups meet, there is a considerable amount of dispute at the territorial boundaries; this involves much vocal signaling and ritualized threat and fighting behavior.

COLOBUS MONKEYS CLASSIFICATION

The colobus monkeys inhabit the forests, woodlands and savannah of equatorial Africa. Members of the subfamily Colobinae, they fall into two groups—the black and the red colobuses. The black colobus monkeys of the genus *Colobus* comprise the guereza, *C. abyssineus*, which occurs over much of Central and East Africa; the black colobus, *C. satanas*, of Gabon, Equatorial Guinea and Cameroon; the Angolan black-and-white colobus, *C. angolensis*, of Angola, southern Zaire, Tanzania and Kenya; and the western black-and-white colobus, *C. polykomos*, of West Africa.

The red colobus monkeys form the genus *Procolobus*. The five species include the red colobus, *P. pennanti*, of Central Africa north and south of the Equator and several outlying areas; the western red colobus, *P. badius*, which occurs in West Africa from Senegal to Ghana; and the olive colobus, *P. verus*, which ranges from Sierra Leone to Nigeria. More than ten subspecies of the red colobus have been described, and some zoologists regard several of these monkeys as separate species.

Langur infanticide

In the areas where population density is high and food resources scarce, it has been observed that young hanuman langurs in a troop may suddenly disappear.

The death of young langurs has been attributed to several possible causes. One theory is that they are killed by an adult male. Another is that they are the victims of cannibalism among the monkeys. Clearly this would drastically reduce the number of mouths to feed—mouths that require special diets and considerable energy expenditure by the mother through the production of milk for suckling. It has also been suggested that the sudden death of the infant blocks the reproductive capacity of many females for a certain period of time and this helps, albeit indirectly, to keep the population within acceptable limits. This seems unlikely to be the case. On the contrary, the removal of an offspring usually has the effect of bringing the female into heat again more quickly than if she had kept her infant.

The population control theory may have some truth in it, as may the suggestion that the stress of overcrowding generates a murderous streak in the adult monkeys, who reduce the stress by slaughtering the young ones.

A new theory

Recent observations, however, have shed some light on the mystery and suggested a different reason for infanticide. The troops, dominated by single males, are under constant threat from lone males and from all-male troops. The male's rule over his harem may be short. He has only to meet a stronger, perhaps younger, competitor to risk being thrown out. When this happens, it seems that the slaughter of the innocents is carried out by the adult male who has recently become the new group leader.

It may be that the purpose of the killing of the infants has to do with reproduction. A male taking over a harem will follow a course of action that will lead to the perpetuation of his genes. In killing the young, he gets rid of hereditary characteristics handed down by his predecessor. Infanticide could, therefore, be a way of promoting his own genes and improving the chances of his genes being handed on to the next generation.

Not all males indulge in infanticide—it is much more common in the densest populations—and not all males are good at it. They often attack the young ones but fail to kill them.

Training for survival

The females will support the leader against challengers, but if the leader does change, the females will act together to protect the young animals. They train their offspring to be survivors from an early age by abandoning them for short and then increasingly long periods to encourage independence. Group responsibility for the young is strengthened by the sharing of the rearing role by other females in the group. Females will even suckle other females' babies. This is not uncommon in the colobines.

Infanticide has been recorded in other monkeys, some only distantly related to the hanuman langur. The process may have similar purposes and may have evolved independently. It is carried out by the blue monkey and by the silvered leaf monkey and also by the New World howler monkeys.

SWINGERS AND CLIMBERS

The apes of Africa and Asia are the primates closest to man in intelligence and perception of the world. They are also physically powerful and have strong family bonds

The apes are the anthropoids closest to human beings in evolutionary terms. They all lack tails, have flattened faces and possess large brains in relation to their body sizes. In habits and social life they show many features reminiscent of human behavior. Unlike humans, however, their arms are generally longer than their legs and are used for getting from one place to another. They are mainly vegetarian and inhabit forests, woodlands and savannah in tropical regions of Africa and Asia.

The two ape families are normally referred to as the lesser apes and the great apes. The former contains the gibbons, including the siamang, while the latter comprises the common and pygmy chimpanzees, the gorillas and the orangutan.

The lesser apes

The gibbons are the smallest of the apes, their body lengths varying from 18 in. to over 3 feet. Their arms and hands are very long, enabling the gibbons to swing easily through the branches of trees in their forest home. When moving in this way—a method of locomotion known as brachiation—they swing alternately using one arm followed by the other, their hands acting as hooks rather than gripping onto the branches. The resulting freedom of movement helps to make them one of the fastest and most agile of all tree-dwelling mammals.

Gibbons have no tails, but they have thick-skinned rump callosities on which they rest when sitting. Their skulls are small and rounded, their snouts are short and their nostrils are widely spaced. Slender and lightly built, the gibbons have short, broad ribcages, and their spines are straight rather than S-shaped as in the other apes and in humans. Though they are

BELOW Siamangs are larger than other gibbons and move more slowly through the trees. They are not as selective in their choice of food as other gibbons, and usually consume whatever is available in one location before moving on to a new feeding site.

PAGE 837 The lar gibbon's long arms enable it to swing at great speed from one branch to another. Collectively known as the lesser apes, the gibbons are classed in a separate family from the chimps, orangutan and gorilla—the so-called great apes.

superbly adapted for brachiating, they can also walk upright more easily than the other apes, both on the ground and on branches.

The diet of gibbons is varied, but they are particularly fond of fruit, which they delicately pick from trees using their fingers and opposable thumbs, first checking the fruit for ripeness. Some small invertebrates are also eaten to provide protein.

Gibbons live in territorial family groups, the adult pair rearing new offspring every two to three years, after a gestation period of about seven months. The young gibbons hang onto their mother's fur at first, and for a long time afterward remain close to their parents. They are not weaned until early in their second year. Sexual maturity is reached at about seven years of age, and the animals are long-lived—in captivity, and apparently in the wild, they can live for up to 30 years.

The siamang

Siamangs are larger than any of their close relatives among the gibbons. They reach about 35 in. in length and over 22 lbs. in weight. Their arms, when stretched wide apart, can reach a span of up to 5 ft. from fingertips to fingertips. A distinctive feature of the siamang is the presence of a thin membrane joining the second and third toes for over half of their length. The animal's fur is long and shiny, and is completely black, except on the eyebrows where it changes to reddish brown. The rest of the face is almost completely hairless and is black in color.

Siamangs inhabit tropical forests and jungles at elevations of up to 5000 ft. They are active during the day, and are almost exclusively arboreal (tree-dwelling), normally occupying a layer of the forest about 100 ft. above the ground. They are monogamous animals, forming long-lasting pair bonds, and live with their offspring in small family groups. Each group has a well-defined territory and a regular sleeping tree. The group spends a lot of time together, especially in grooming, and, even when feeding separately, family members rarely stray more than a few yards from each other. Single siamangs also occur—these are probably young animals that have left the family group but have not yet paired.

The siamang has a large vocal organ—a pink or gray throat sac that is inflated during calling. Like all the gibbons, the siamang indulges in elaborate and

ABOVE The siamang's large throat sac—a bag of loose, naked skin—becomes swollen with air during the animal's calling sessions. Its cries commence in the early morning just after dawn, when pairs of adult siamangs engage in loud duets that can be heard over a mile away. Though the sessions undoubtedly serve to advertise the presence of a siamang family and confirm their occupation of a territory, they probably also help to strengthen and maintain the bond between the adults.

APES AND HUMANS CLASSIFICATION

Two families among the primates are known as apes. The siamang and the gibbons belong to the family Hylobatidae, the lesser apes; the chimpanzees, the orangutan and the gorillas belong to the family Pongidae, the great apes. Humans are the only living representatives of the family Hominidae, although our closest fossil ancestors are also considered to be part of the group. The great apes and humans are sometimes regarded as close enough in form to be combined in a superfamily called the Hominoidea.

ABOVE The range of the siamang in Malaysia and Sumatra is continually being cut back as the rain forests are cleared for agriculture and, especially, to provide timber for the logging industry. In the mid-1970s, the animal's total population was estimated at less than 200,000, and scientists predicted that within a few decades only isolated populations would be left, assuming that the pressures from land clearance continue.

energetic calling sessions. The loud "songs" serve to define territory, and almost certainly have another role in confirming, strengthening and perhaps even celebrating the pair bond between the adults. The male produces a scream, while the female utters a series of barks that lasts up to 20 seconds. The calls are made particularly vibrant by the sound of the air being forced out of the vocal sac. A deeper, booming sound results if air is drawn in through the nostrils while the mouth is kept closed.

The zoologist John MacKinnon, who carried out extensive research on the songs of the gibbons, confirmed that the siamangs' cries act as territorial proclamations. One day, he and his colleagues had finished recording the calls of a group of siamangs they were studying deep in the jungle, and they had the idea of playing back the recorded calls to the group. Three distraught faces immediately poked through the leaves above the researchers' heads. Then the siamangs started to bound off in different directions, running to and fro across their territory, confused by the recordings of their own territorial announcements.

Competition among species

Territories belonging to siamang family groups often overlap with the territories of other gibbons that inhabit the same environment. Several monkey species, including macaques and colobines, also frequent the same habitat. In practice, however, the siamangs only compete with the gibbons, since they eat a similar diet—though the siamangs tend to eat more leaves and insects, while the gibbons concentrate more on fruit.

Though the potential for competition between gibbons and siamangs is great, their different habits normally prevent them from meeting at feeding sites. Gibbons wake up earlier in the morning and by the time the siamangs arrive, they have usually finished feeding. Conversely, when siamangs are the first to find a tree loaded with ripe fruit, they will not generally allow the smaller gibbons to approach until they have eaten their fill.

Foraging strategies

Another important difference between the siamang and other gibbons lies in their different foraging strategies. According to MacKinnon, siamangs only cover about half a mile a day on average and stop up to eight times to feed. Gibbons, on the other hand, regularly cover twice the distance and will stop to eat over 16 times in one day. Over a period of five days, a siamang family obtained 50 percent of its food intake from the fruit of three trees, whereas the gibbon families visited at least 10 trees.

By continually monitoring the trees and climbing plants within a small area (especially the various species of wild figs—one of their favorite foods), a siamang family learns when and where it can find the best ripe fruit. Their intimacy with their feeding territory, combined with the fact that they are dominant over smaller species of gibbons, means that the siamangs can obtain more, better-quality fruit from a limited area than they could if they ranged farther afield.

SWINGERS AND CLIMBERS

The siamang is territorial and monogamous (it has only one mate at a time). Males and females mate for life, although they may make a few false starts before finding a permanent partner. They live in family groups of up to six animals. Such small units are typical of the gibbons, and are in distinct contrast to the large societies formed by the many species of Old World monkeys.

Zoologists have speculated on the reason for the small size of these groups. According to one theory, it is the result of diet. All the gibbon species—and the siamangs in particular—specialize in finding, selecting and gathering ripe fruit, which is more nutritious than tough, fibrous leaves. But fruit is a scarce resource in the forest, compared to the abundant leaves and shoots that form the staple diet of most monkeys. As a result, the forest is able to support fewer fruit foragers than leaf eaters. (Certain macaques do eat great quantities of fruit when they can find it, but they do not depend on it.)

Compatible eaters

A study carried out in one small section of Malaysian forest lends some support to this theory. The area studied contained only 12 individual gibbons (including siamangs), but over 150 monkeys of three species. Clearly, it would have been impractical for the apes to compete for food with such a number of monkeys. While the monkeys fed on the leaves and unripe fruit, the gibbons concentrated on the ripe fruit hanging from branches that often lay beyond the reach of the less agile monkeys.

The scarcity of fruit puts a limit not only on the number of gibbons in any one part of the forest, but also on the number that can forage together. Gibbons

BELOW Gripping the branch beneath with its long toes, a gibbon searches among the foliage for ripe fruit. Most gibbons are specialist fruit eaters, and since ripe fruit is a scarce resource, its supply limits the number of gibbons that can forage together. They normally feed in family groups of four to six, keeping to their own patch of the forest and uttering loud calls as a warning to other gibbons.

ABOVE The arms of gibbons are almost as long as their legs and bodies combined, making it difficult for them to walk on all fours on the ground. Instead, the gibbons raise their arms above their heads and move about on two legs.

GIBBONS CLASSIFICATION

The nine species of gibbons all belong to the family Hylobatidae, and are considered by most zoologists to comprise a single genus—*Hylobates*. They are all forest animals and range over Indonesia and Southeast Asia.

The siamang, *H. syndactylus,* occurs in mainland Malaysia and in Sumatra. The lar or white-handed gibbon, *H. lar,* occurs in Thailand, the Malay Peninsula and northern Sumatra, while the closely related agile gibbon, *H. agilis,* lives in Sumatra and in parts of Thailand, Malaysia and Borneo; the moloch gibbon, *H. moloch,* in western Java; and Muller's gibbon, *H. Muelleri,* in all parts of Borneo except the southwest. The rarest and most threatened gibbons are the kloss gibbon, *H. klossii,* found only in the Mentawai Islands off the west coast of Sumatra; the concolor or crested gibbon, *H. concolor,* of southeast China, Laos, Vietnam, parts of Kampuchea and Hainan; the hoolock gibbon, *H. hoolock,* of Bangladesh, Assam, Burma and adjacent parts of China; and the pileated gibbon, *H. pileatus,* of southeast Thailand and Kampuchea west of the Mekong.

and siamangs that form groups of four or more have to cover much more ground each day and be satisfied with a much smaller proportion of fruit in their diet than those animals that form groups of two or three. In other words, by having an extra mouth to feed, the larger gibbon group has to travel farther afield, and use up more energy to find the same amount of fruit per individual. Gibbons have therefore restricted the size of the foraging groups to a maximum of six individuals—and the family group represents the best way of keeping to this limit. Each family vigorously defends its feeding territory against other gibbons, ensuring its own local supply of fruit.

Territorial song

For a gibbon, the best way of defending its territory is to advertise its presence by using the voice. Like the howler monkeys of South America, gibbons produce loud, characteristic calls that help each group keep track of its neighbors, and warn them off their territory. The calls are elaborate and often musical. The siamang has evolved an inflatable throat sac that acts as a sound chamber, enhancing the resonance and the carrying power of their calls.

Pairs of adult gibbons defend their territory by "singing" in duets. On the Mentawai Islands, off the west coast of Sumatra, Indonesia, pairs of kloss gibbons defend an area of 49-86 acres (large enough for a family of four) by "singing" for an hour or so just before dawn. The calls are answered by those of neighboring apes, enabling the animals to assert

rights over their patch of forest. The song is also a means of determining the status of one animal over another. The animals rarely meet for a show of strength; instead, they try to out-sing each other.

It is important for an acrobatic animal like the gibbon that status is not determined by strength. If it were, the larger individuals would be the most successful. Males would then tend to be bigger than females and less agile among the branches (as is the case with orangutans). As it is, strength and size are not the determining factor; male and female gibbons are of similar size and are equally acrobatic.

Female songs

Female kloss gibbons produce dramatic calls made up of repeated rising and falling notes. These reach a climax in a loud, resonant trill, uttered as the animal hurls herself through the branches, sending broken foliage and dead wood crashing to the forest floor. She does this every three or four days, apparently warning other females to stay away from her mate.

Attention seekers

The rest of the family may join in with this display of the female's, calling and waving severed branches. The sense of belonging that this encourages may help to strengthen the family bonds, and prevent the male from courting other females. Since the male kloss gibbon shows little interest in his offspring, and tends to forage apart from the rest of the family group, he could quite easily become distracted by any unattached

ABOVE Few primates can compete with the gibbon when it comes to agility in the trees. With its long, powerful arms, strong fingers and shortened thumbs, it is superbly adapted to swinging from branch to branch. It moves with such grace and confidence that it seems incapable of making a mistake, yet broken bones are common among gibbons.
BELOW The gibbon's agility demands a slight build. Here a male gibbon (A) is compared with a male orangutan (B), chimpanzee (C) and gorilla (D).

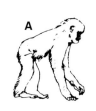

THE LAR GIBBONS
— AERIAL ACROBATS OF SOUTHEAST ASIA —

The lar gibbon of Malaysia and Sumatra is one of the most colorful of the gibbon family. It always has a ring of white fur surrounding its naked, dark-skinned face, but its body color ranges from buff through red and dark brown to black.

Lar gibbons live in family groups of up to six members (although four is the average), the group being made up of a mature pair and their young. The groups can often be recognized by similarities in their coat coloration. Lone lars are sometimes observed— usually young males that have outgrown the group, but have yet to start families of their own.

Each group occupies its own patch of forest, asserting its rights by regular loud, musical calls. These calls alert other gibbons to their presence— something not always obvious in the thick forest foliage—and warns them to keep clear. In this way, each family maintains a virtual monopoly of the ripe fruit in its immediate area, making long journeys in search of food unnecessary.

Family quarrels

Although the calling reduces disputes between different groups of gibbons, aggressive encounters between the individuals in one group cannot be avoided. Quarrels over food are a common source of conflict within a family. When young adults leave their family group to start an independent life, it is partly aggression from their parents (from which parent depends on the species) that gradually drives them away. The "eviction" of sub-adults ensures that there is sufficient food for new offspring, and it keeps the population density in line with the amount of food available. However, the sub-adults also leave partly because they are ready to start their own breeding families.

A perilous nursery

Newborn gibbons have an alarming start in life, forced to endure being carried at dizzying speed across the treetops. They immediately cling to their mothers' bellies, both day and night, regardless of her acrobatics

through the trees. In captivity, young gibbons often die when they lose their grip on their mother's fur, and although it is not known how often this happens in the wild, dead gibbons of all ages are occasionally found on the forest floor. Agile though they are, there is always the chance that a gibbon progressing through the trees will pick a rotten branch that snaps as soon as it grips it, and one out of four adults show signs of fractured limbs.

Strength in the arms

Gibbons have developed particularly powerful arm muscles that enable them to swing hand over hand from branch to branch. Their hands have become like grapnel hooks, perfectly adapted to latching onto branches as the animal hurtles through the air. The thumbs are short and are separated from the other four fingers so as not to obstruct the swift, hook-like action of the hands. Having such short thumbs makes it hard for the animal to grip small objects. To make up for this, their long big toes are better suited to precision work, and a gibbon's hind foot resembles a man's hand more closely than its forefoot. The line of evolution that produced the gibbons emphasized their agility in the trees over their dexterity. As a result, they have become the most specialized of all tree-dwelling primates.

LEFT Ranging through Thailand, Malaysia and northern Sumatra, the lar gibbon remains one of the more numerous of the gibbons, but continued deforestation threatens to reduce and fragment their population. ABOVE RIGHT AND RIGHT Ranging in color from black to pale buff, lars are the most variable of the gibbons. Though both sexes in any one area are usually of similar shade, detailed coloring differs from one individual to another. The gibbons themselves may use coat coloration to recognize each other at a distance, although it is often difficult to see far through the dense tropical foliage.

female who entered the territory, so the resident female has every reason to be cautious.

The male siamang has a much stronger natural bond with his young than does the male gibbon. The siamang looks after his offspring, carries them around on his shoulders and seems to gain great satisfaction from the relationship. Behavior of this sort is not confined to siamangs. Several South American primates, such as the titi monkeys, act in the same way. In the Old World, certain male baboons and Barbary macaques will sometimes strike up a friendship with younger animals of their own species, although rarely with their own offspring. In these cases, the young animal seems to act as a social prop or support for the older male, who apparently gains status from the presence of a devoted disciple. In siamangs, the situation is more straightforward: the adult males show paternal affection within a very tightly knit family unit.

Aerial grace

Most gibbons are smaller and more elegant than siamangs, and are the most accomplished of all the apes when it comes to moving through the trees. Their arms are longer in proportion to their bodies, giving them a considerable turn of speed as they swing through the trees, hand over hand. Their movements are so fluid and graceful that they seem to glide from branch to branch. When walking along branches, gibbons hold their arms up in the air, reminiscent of tightrope walkers who spread their arms for balance. Even on the ground, gibbons walk upright like humans.

Coats of many colors

The coat colors of all gibbons—apart from the siamang, kloss gibbon and moloch gibbon—vary from one population to another. In some species there may be a variation of coat color between the sexes. In the concolor gibbon of eastern Southeast Asia, the males are black with whitish, or sometimes reddish, cheeks. The females have golden or buff (dull yellow) coats, sometimes with black patches. The male has a tuft of hair on top of its head, giving it a pointed look, whereas the female has two much shorter tufts that give its head a more square-cut look.

The male hoolock gibbons that inhabit Burma and Bangladesh are always colored deep black, while the females vary from brown to gray. The pileated gibbon

ABOVE The gibbon's light build gives it an advantage over heavyweight apes like the orangutan, for it can reach the very tips of slender branches to pick the fruit that grows there. In some areas gibbons and orangutans feed quite amicably in the same tree, with the gibbons taking the fruit farthest from reach and the orangutans gathering food nearer the large branches. Such variations in feeding habits explain why animals will often tolerate other species, but chase off their own kind.

Lar gibbon

Pygmy chimpanzee

Common chimpanzee

Orangutan

Siamang

Gorilla

ABOVE The orangutan of Borneo and Sumatra is a slow-moving, solitary animal that feeds mainly on ripe fruit. Its name is a Malay word meaning "man of the woods."
BELOW The world map shows the distribution of the great and lesser apes.

of Thailand and Kampuchea also varies in color according to sex: females are silver-gray with black cheeks, cap and chest, but males have black coats and white hands and feet. ("Pileus" in Latin means "felt cap," hence the adjective "pileated.")

Distinctive hands

The lar or white-handed gibbon of Thailand and Sumatra varies in color according to the race it belongs to. In one locality, the males and females may all be red; in another they may all be black. Color variations also include light or dark buff and brown. The backs of their hands and feet are always white. The agile gibbon of Sumatra, Borneo and the Malay Peninsula is similar in appearance to the lar, having the same color variations, but its hands and feet are always dark on top. Muller's gibbon, found in northeast Borneo, varies from brown to gray; the moloch gibbon of western Java is always silver-gray in both sexes.

The differences in color and habits among the gibbons seem to have arisen as a result of geographical isolation. In most cases, the various species are cut off from one another by stretches of water—either seas or large rivers. It is probable that when they first colonized Southeast Asia these barriers did not exist, and all gibbons were much the same. Subsequent

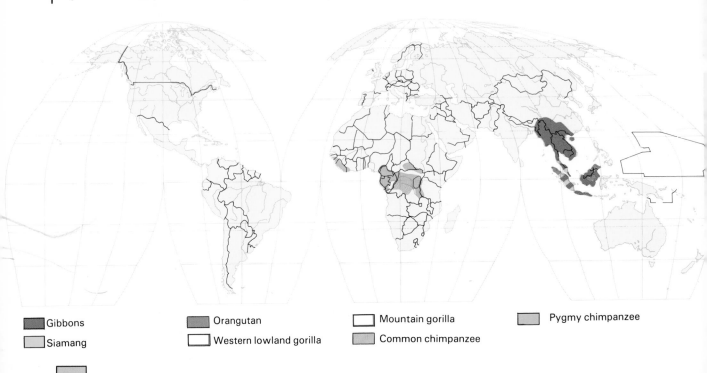

☐ Gibbons
☐ Siamang
☐ Orangutan
☐ Western lowland gorilla
☐ Mountain gorilla
☐ Common chimpanzee
☐ Pygmy chimpanzee

LEFT **Though they are more sociable than orangutans, chimpanzees usually split up when foraging for fruit. Mature females are often accompanied by their young—infants are allowed to ride on their mothers' backs or shoulders until they are fully weaned.**

ABOVE **The gorilla feeds mainly on the ground-level leaves of herbs, shrubs and vines, but it also consumes ripe fruit.**
PAGES 850-851 **A young orangutan needs to keep a tight grip on its mother in case she is suddenly alarmed and heads for the treetops.**

changes in sea level isolated the surviving populations from one another, and they developed separately into the species that exist today. Unfortunately, the continuing exploitation of the forest has reduced their habitat to a fraction of its former extent, and several gibbons are now on the endangered list.

The great apes

Although gibbons have many human-like features (such as their expressive faces and habit of walking upright) they are not as closely related to man as the great apes. These—the orangutan, the two species of chimpanzee, and the biggest of all, the gorillas—are probably the most familiar of all the primates, and certainly the most spectacular.

Fossils of both lesser and great apes have been found in rocks dating from 20 million years ago. The modern orangutan is very similar to these early great apes. Chimpanzees and gorillas show a number of more advanced features, and lead a different way of life, being essentially ground-living animals rather than tree dwellers like the orangutan and the gibbons. It is probable that the chimpanzees and gorillas developed more recently, at about the same time that the first humans appeared some 10-15 million years ago.

Slow-moving orangs

Despite living on the ground, both chimpanzees and gorillas have retained the long arms of animals adapted to swinging through the trees. (In some areas, both chimpanzees and gorillas spend a good deal of time feeding in the trees.) In fact, they are too heavy to hurl themselves from branch to branch like the

The apes occur in West and Central Africa, southern China, Southeast Asia and Indonesia.

gibbons, although young, lighter animals may swing with their arms for short periods. Orangutans, the only real tree dwellers in the family, move slowly from branch to branch using all four limbs to support their often considerable weight. They use their weight to bend one branch or tree down toward another, moving across and letting the bent branch sweep back with a crash of foliage. Orangutans have extremely flexible joints, and the animals often rest in positions that, to our eyes, look very uncomfortable.

On the ground, chimpanzees and gorillas walk on all fours, resting their forelimbs on the knuckles of their hands. As a result, they have thick calluses on the middle joints of their fingers. On the ground, orangutans support themselves on the outer edges of their hands, giving them an awkward gait. It is usually the larger male orangutans that come down to the forest floor, possibly because their greater weight makes movement through the trees more difficult.

Similar to humans

Apes, like humans, rely heavily on acquired skills rather than instinct. They achieve maturity slowly, and the young apes depend on their mothers for several years—giving them plenty of time to learn about the ways of ape society and the skills of survival before striking out on their own.

Female apes become sexually mature at about the age of eight years, whereas many female monkeys achieve maturity at about four. Among both monkeys and apes, sexual and social maturity amount to the same thing: in primate societies the female acquires her status in the group when her first offspring is born. Before that she is treated as an adjunct of her mother, and during this immature period she has plenty of time to watch, listen and learn.

Tools and weapons

One human-like skill that is common among chimpanzees is the ability to use tools. In some populations, they use rocks and big sticks as hammers to split tough-skinned fruit, and small sticks as probes to collect ants and termites from their nests. Males may also brandish sticks and stones when they are putting on a threat display, and may even use them as weapons in hunting. For unlike the other great apes, chimpanzees prey on other mammals. The use of tools and weapons was once thought to be a purely human characteristic, but the fact that chimpanzees and many other animal species use them has shown this to be untrue.

Communicaton is another area where the great apes display human-like characteristics. They have developed an elaborate vocabulary of visual and vocal signals that enables them to express their intentions and emotions with accuracy. Attempts to teach chimpanzees the rudiments of speech or sign language have met with a certain degree of success.

The orangutan

Although not the largest of the primates, the orangutan is surely one of the most distinctive. It is a tree-dwelling ape with immensely long arms—a big male may have an arm span of six feet or more—from which hang shaggy fringes of long, chestnut hair. Mature males have throat pouches and projections of fatty tissue around their bearded faces, giving them a mask-like appearance meant to intimidate other males during territorial confrontations. The throat pouch

——— GREAT APES ——— CLASSIFICATION

Of the four great apes in the family Pongidae, three are native to Africa. The common chimpanzee, *Pan troglodytes,* is the most widespread, occupying forest and grassland near wooded areas throughout West and Central Africa and as far east as Tanzania. The pygmy chimpanzee or bonobo, *Pan paniscus,* is limited to the forests of Zaire in Central Africa.

The gorilla, *Gorilla gorilla,* consists of three subspecies. The western lowland gorilla, *G. g. gorilla,* lives in the tropical forest of coastal Central Africa, mainly in Cameroon, Gabon and Congo, while the eastern lowland gorilla, *G. g. graueri,* is found in the forests of eastern Zaire. The very rare mountain gorilla, *G. g. beringei,* lives in bamboo and rain forests in the Virunga mountain range along the borders of Zaire, Uganda and Rwanda.

The orangutan, *Pongo pygmaeus,* is the only Asian member of the great apes. Now endangered, it occurs in the tropical forests of lowland Borneo and northern Sumatra, the Bornean population forming the subspecies *P. p. pygmaeus* and the Sumatran the subspecies *P. p. abelii.*

can be inflated with air to act as a resonator, adding volume to the male's territorial calls.

Males are much bigger than females, weighing 198 lbs. or more in comparison to a female's 88-110 lbs. The orangutan's status is measured by strength, bulk and an impressive appearance: the bigger the male, the more status he has. Higher status brings greater success in breeding, with the result that a high proportion of the orangutans born each year are fathered by large males and inherit their fathers' bulk.

While the male orangutan's heavyweight frame is useful as a means of scaring off competition, it is a definite handicap when it comes to moving about in the trees. The fluid movements of a smaller primate such as a gibbon are quite beyond the ability of a big male. The male orangutans come down to ground level much more frequently. Indeed, all orangutans, male and female, move slowly and laboriously through the branches, clinging on with all four limbs. Like all apes, orangutans are tailless.

Two populations

Once widespread across Southeast Asia, orangutans are now restricted to the moist rain forests of Borneo and Sumatra. The two populations were almost certainly separated from each other several thousand years ago, but there are no major differences between them—a practiced eye, however, would be able to distinguish the two races. As with many tree-dwelling primates, they are vulnerable to the destruction of their forest habitat, and they are now an endangered species.

Orangutans eat a wide range of food, including young leaves and shoots, insects, small mammals and reptiles, but most of the time they eat fruit. They have strong jaws and big teeth for ripping open fruit husks and tearing off the tree bark that forms an occasional supplement to their diet. Big males are capable of eating huge quantities of fruit at one sitting, and often stay at a favored site for several hours. Females, being more agile, move around more and take several snacks throughout the day. Orangutans do their foraging during the day, spending their nights in nests made from broken branches and foliage.

Unusual for apes, orangutans are quite often solitary by nature. Adults live separately and forage alone, unless they are females with young; but even juvenile orangutans leave their mothers and go off on

ABOVE Unlike gibbons that swing from their forelimbs, orangutans hold on to branches with both their arms and their legs. Their limbs are so similar in structure that the animals could be mistaken for having four arms. Even lightweight orangutans such as this juvenile use the all-fours technique, although they could swing by one hand, if necessary, from the tougher branches. Mature males are so heavy that they have little option but to hang on to as many of the supporting branches as they can.

ABOVE Young orangutans of either sex look much the same (left), but as they get older, differences between the females (center) and the males (right) become more pronounced. The males grow much larger, reaching almost twice the weight of the females.

They also develop prominent throat sacs and face flanges, which in old, overweight individuals become swollen with fat.

BELOW An orangutan demonstrates how it keeps a firm grip on the branches with three of its limbs as it reaches out to pick a fruit.

Bellowing calls

Orangutans frequently greet each other with apparent indifference. The powerful males, however, have their breeding interests to consider, and advertise their presence with a drawn-out bellowing call. This tells other male orangutans where they are and warns them to keep their distance. (It may also attract females that are ready to mate.) If two big males do meet, they intimidate one another by displaying their bulk, breaking branches and lumbering around. Ultimately, they may resort to violence, biting and scratching at each other. One male usually backs down before things get to this stage, but most wild males bear the scars of their aggressive encounters.

The defensive behavior of orangutans is very important to the animals because the opportunities to mate are so few and far between. Most females breed, on average, every five years. They may be sexually active for several months before becoming pregnant, but after that they are unreceptive until the young are off their hands—a period of seven years or so. The female's slow rate of breeding makes it necessary for the dominant male to mate with as many females as possible.

Finding a mate

To catch the females during their sexually receptive period, and to stop other males from getting to them, the male orangutan has to extend his breeding territory to include the home ranges of several females. He will then drive away any rival males who may cross the boundaries. Once all the females in the area are pregnant, an ambitious male may well move on to another patch of the forest in the hope of finding more females with whom he can mate. The male naturally comes into conflict with resident males, and this is the most common cause of fights.

Young competitors

Despite all his efforts, an adult male does not always enjoy a monopoly of the females within his area. He has priority in theory, but in practice his bulk and clumsiness often provide opportunities for younger more agile males to slip in, mate with receptive females and make off before the resident male can get to them. Male orangutans become sexually mature at about 10 years old, but they do not reach their full size until they are 15 years. As a result, there are always plenty of young males waiting for an opportunity to

their own while still immature. Each animal occupies its own feeding range of several square miles. These overlap with the ranges of other orangutans, but border disputes over feeding grounds are rare. On the contrary, neighboring orangutans may converge on a heavily laden fruit tree, fill themselves with fruit, and leave without taking any notice of each other.

One reason that the orangutans are solitary feeders is the large proportion of fruit in their diet. Fruit is a relatively scarce commodity in the forest—compared with leaves—and a troop of orangutans would have to travel several miles each day to find enough fruit to satisfy them all. Limits on the size of foraging groups affects gibbons, too, but since gibbons are smaller, each individual requires less food and the animals can afford to forage together in their small family units.

For a large animal like an orangutan, it is better to forage alone, since an individual can usually track down enough fruit to satisfy its own appetite within a small area. By traveling only short distances to find their food, they are able to save energy. Orangutans have no trouble in finding trees with ripe fruit on them; they appear to have a thorough knowledge of the local trees, and they even watch the movements of fruit-eating birds to track down the fruit.

ABOVE Orangutans breed infrequently—in the wild, it is normal for a female to give birth only once every five years. The mother treats each infant with great care, suckling it for three years and often keeping it by her until the next infant is born. Single births are the rule; twins, such as those shown above, are a rare event. FAR RIGHT Gorillas are the most powerful of the apes, with massively muscled chests, necks and arms. The adult males attain such a weight that only the stoutest of trees can support their bulk if they climb above the ground.

The gorilla is the giant among the anthropoids. The males may weigh up to 606 lbs. or more and reach about 6 ft. in height. The females are much smaller than the males, reaching about 5 ft. when standing upright, and weighing around 198 lbs. Both sexes are tailless. A male's head has a different shape than the female's, with a pronounced crest formed by a ridge of bone running along the top of the skull.

The ridge of bone on the skull forms an anchor for the powerful jaw muscles. In females the muscles are not as powerful, and the ridge of bone is much smaller or even absent. Males also have longer canine teeth that they use as weapons on the rare occasions when confrontations between males develop into fights. Both sexes are heavily built, with broad chests and muscular arms and legs.

Coat color

The gorilla's thick coat is basically very dark and varies in color according to the subspecies. In the eastern form it is a uniform jet black, whereas there are brownish gray tints in the coat of the western form. The mountain gorilla has jet black fur, which is longer than in the other two subspecies, especially on the top of the head and on the arms. With age, adult males develop a silvery-white saddle of hair on their backs which is larger in the western lowland gorilla.

The faces, chests, hands and feet of gorillas are virtually hairless. They have broad, fleshy nostrils, small ears almost hidden by fur, and pronounced eyebrow ridges that make their eyes look smaller than they really are.

There are three subspecies of gorillas, found in two densely forested areas of Central Africa. The western lowland gorilla lives in equatorial Africa to the north and west of the Zaire (or Congo) River. The mountain gorilla and the eastern lowland gorilla occur in the uplands and lowlands respectively of eastern Zaire, Rwanda and Uganda.

There can be little doubt that at one time the distribution of gorillas was continuous across Central Africa, but the three populations have become cut off from one another by vast tracts of primary forest—now becoming increasingly fragmented—that does not suit them. They prefer the more open, secondary forest that has regrown where primary forest has at some time been cut down. Secondary forest suits their terrestrial (ground-dwelling) life-style and their

mate. Eventually the old males are replaced by younger rivals. When this happens, the old males go off on their own and rarely attempt to mate again.

Orangutans usually mate in a tree. The pair often stay together for several days, mating repeatedly. Sometimes the male asserts himself over the female against her will, but at other times the two seem to be equally enthusiastic. On occasions, the female may even initiate the mating.

The peaceful gorilla

Few animals have been more misrepresented than the gorilla. Massive, powerful and intimidating in appearance, it has long been regarded as a ferocious animal. But in truth it is a gentle, peaceful creature, and one of the most intelligent of all the primates.

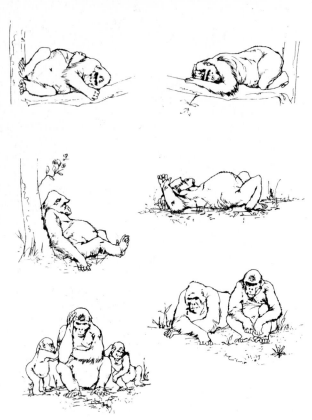

ABOVE **The huge bulk and intimidating display behavior of male gorillas have earned them a reputation for savagery that is quite unjustified. A gorilla will only attack a human if it feels that its** family **is being threatened in some way.**
LEFT **In the midday heat gorillas stop foraging for food and rest in the shade. There, they either sleep, groom one another, or watch the infants playing.**

vegetarian habits; there are far more food plants growing on the floor of an open, secondary forest than there are in the shady depths of primary forests.

In areas where trees and vines are abundant, gorillas climb a good deal and feed high up in the trees, though the height at which they feed varies according to the geographical area. The Zaire River flows between the two gorilla areas and this may have played a role in keeping the populations separate. Gorillas have an instinctive dislike of water and will not cross a stream or river unless boulders or branches form a natural bridge.

Ancient skins

The gorilla has been known to Western science for a long time. The first gorilla skins were brought back from Central Africa in 460 BC by the Carthaginian explorer Hanno. His expedition sailed up the Niger River for some distance, and apparently encountered

gorillas during its explorations of the surrounding forests. According to the Roman author Pliny the Elder (AD 23-79), the Romans saw some gorilla skins when they conquered Carthage in 146 BC. There they also learned the name that had been given to this unusual creature by the Carthaginians: "gorilla" (thought to have derived from an African language and meaning "wild man").

For several centuries gorillas had a more or less mythical status, but toward the end of the 16th century the gorilla and chimpanzee were described in detail by an English navigator who was held prisoner for several years in Portuguese West Africa. Three hundred years passed before live gorillas were seen in Europe. The first arrived at the end of the 19th century. They survived for about two weeks—a sad indication of things to come, for gorillas do not take readily to life behind bars.

Gorillas were not successfully bred in captivity until a few years ago, and for every zoo specimen on display today, it is estimated that at least two have died on the journey from the jungle to the ape house. This poses a real problem, for gorillas are under threat in the wild, and captive breeding programs may prove essential to their survival.

A gentle giant

The legends of the ferocity of gorillas reached a peak in 1933 with the release of the film "King Kong." However, the patient researches of the American primatologists George and Kay Schaller have gone a long way to discrediting this reputation. In 1959 they began two years of close observation of gorillas in the wild, and their revelations changed the public image of this most majestic of primates. They described the gorilla just as they observed them: retiring, placid and predominantly vegetarian animals with a keen sense of family responsibility. Indeed, on the rare occasions when gorillas have shown aggression toward people, it has usually been in defense of their families.

Gorillas—with the exception of young solitary males who have not started breeding—live in harems of several females, their young, and a single mature silverback male. The group may stay together for years, foraging for food and sleeping in nests of broken branches and leaves, and cooperating in the rearing of their offspring. They are able to live in family groups like this because they primarily eat

ABOVE Many gorillas live in areas where the undergrowth is thick and there are plenty of leaves that can be gathered from ground level. They are usually found in open forest, where gaps in the tree cover allow the light to penetrate to the forest floor and encourage the growth of ground vegetation. They cannot live in areas of mature forest where all the trees have to grow tall in order to reach the light, and for this reason, gorillas do not inhabit much of the forested areas of Central Africa.

LEFT Female gorillas breed more frequently than orangutans, but a high infant mortality rate means that nearly half the gorillas that are born fail to survive their first three years. When young, they are like human babies—entirely dependent on their parents.

ABOVE Adult females have little interest in other adult gorillas, but concentrate on feeding and grooming their infants (A). Young gorillas are more sociable and often play together (B). Through their play they learn the basics of social behavior.

foliage, which is an abundant source of food. In contrast, the large fruit-eating ape, the orangutan, cannot afford to share the limited quantity of fruit that grows within its range with the rest of its family. It has to forage alone in order to find enough food. Gorillas also eat fruit when they can find it, particularly in the western part of their range.

Chest beaters

Young, agile gorillas will swing through the branches to reach succulent foliage, and even the largest mature male silverbacks may climb to feed at times, despite their great weight. Gorillas rarely travel far when foraging. Moreover, the abundance of their food means that there is no need to defend it. Only when a rival threatens the family group does the harem male resort to his famous chest-beating threat display.

The Schallers pointed out that the chest beating, branch shaking and throwing of leaves and broken wood toward the adversary during threat displays are common to other primates that spend most of their time in the trees, such as the orangutan and the gibbons. The peculiar impressiveness of the gorilla's performance owes a lot to the fact that it takes place on the ground, clear of tangled branches.

A silverback chief

Unlike chimpanzees, which live in fairly flexible social groupings, gorillas form groups that remain relatively stable for long periods. The groups are formed around—and are led by—one dominant male. The group leader is often known as the "silverback" from his striking silver saddle, which develops as he matures. Being bulky animals, gorillas generally lead a

fairly sedentary life (they spend a lot of time sitting and resting), and do not normally patrol or defend their patches. Even so, they do have well-defined home ranges that may extend from 2 to 11.5 square miles and between which there may be a fair degree of overlap. When encounters take place between groups there is rarely any conflict.

Although gorillas are not often aggressive, males may occasionally fight. This happens most frequently when the dominant male of a group meets and is challenged by a single, probably younger male. The females watch as the males roar, scream and beat their chests during the fight for dominance. The group leader will fight to retain his group, and the challenger will take it over if he wins. Even if he doesn't win, one or more of the females may be sufficiently impressed to leave the group and join the young challenger.

Wandering males

Groups are not the only social element. Young males leave the group in which they were born of their own accord—only rarely do they leave as a result of being driven out by the silverback. They will wander alone, perhaps for years, before gathering and leading a group of females and their offspring. When the leader of a group changes—if the patriarch (the father and ruler) dies or becomes too old to maintain control, or if he is successfully challenged—his place is unlikely to be taken by a youngster from within his own group. The new boss is far more likely to be a silverback that has lived alone for some time, but has kept visual contact with the group.

Females, too, leave their family group on attaining maturity at about seven years of age, and usually join a lone young male or a small group rather than teaming up with a larger, well-established group.

Among most of the other social primates, there is a crucial pattern of relationships between the females of the group. These may be of a friendly or argumentative

ABOVE RIGHT AND RIGHT The contrast between the infant gorilla's head shape (above right) and the more rugged and robust adult head (right) is marked. Scientists who study animal behavior have established that the rounded head shape and small, soft features of the infant's face stimulate tender, protective behavior in the adult. The stimulus ensures that the young animal will be protected not only by its own parents but also by other adults within the group.

nature, but in all cases they involve a large degree of social interaction (especially grooming). Such "sisterhood" does not exist in gorilla groups. But while the females have little to do with each other, they will lavish much attention on the group leader. Mutual grooming, for example, rarely occurs between adult females, but they each groom the male and he in turn grooms them. He also grooms the infant gorillas and allows them to play around him. The dominant male gorilla is the most important figure in the whole group, and his decisions and moods decide how the gorillas will spend each day.

A diet of greens

Gorillas are almost exclusively vegetarian. Their diet consists chiefly of stems and leaves, although they are also tempted by several kinds of ripe fruit. Gorillas will climb trees to get the best pick of the fruit, but they spend most of their lives on the ground. The younger animals are more at home in the trees than their elders; older gorillas are heavy and cumbersome, and their bulk prevents them from testing all but the strongest branches.

Despite their weight, gorillas build nests in the trees a few yards off the ground—sometimes actually on the ground—in which to sleep at night. Every evening,

ABOVE The behavior of mountain gorillas has been closely studied by a number of biologists who have found that these gentle giants are easy to study in the wild. Researchers—and any other humans that approach wild gorillas—are first subjected to an intimidatory display, but they are soon accepted by the entire group if it is clear that they do not pose a threat.

each animal builds a fresh nest of twigs, leaves and branches. Gorillas also practice what could be considered a primitive form of conservation. They never completely denude an area of its vegetation before moving on, but leave sufficient vegetation to ensure that it will regrow quickly, regaining its former lushness once they have gone. They can then return later, when the forest has recovered, to feed again in the same area.

Complementary life-styles

In Africa's forests, much of the available food—leaves, flowers and fruit in particular—is found in the higher levels of vegetation. As a result, most rain forest animals are arboreal (tree dwellers) and exploit the abundance and the diversity of the food that grows there. The gorilla, however, has evolved to occupy a different habitat. Thousands of years ago, competition with its smaller, more agile relative, the chimpanzee, probably forced the gorilla to exploit a different food source within the same forest environment. In this way the two species are complementary to one another, rather than competitors. The slower pace and greater bulk of the gorillas, which came about through its adaptation to a ground-dwelling life-style, helped to shape the social behavior of gorilla groups.

Gorillas became vegetarian only recently in evolutionary terms, and their ability to digest vegetable matter, particularly leaves and grass, is still not perfect. Some undigested matter remains in the feces after the food has passed through the gorilla's system.

The chimpanzees

Of all the apes, chimpanzees are best known to the general public since they are the species most frequently captured and kept in zoos. Their endearing appearance and lively intelligence have sometimes

RIGHT When danger threatens, gorilla groups are defended only by the dominant male in the clan. There are reports that even if he is killed, the females will make little attempt to defend themselves.
BELOW The different stages of a threat display: the male pretends to eat as it observes an intruder (A); pulls up grass and twigs (B); beats his chest (C); stamps on the ground (D); pulls up more grass and walks from side to side (E); and beats the ground with his hand (F). If the intruder still does not move, the gorilla will either retreat or, more rarely, will attack.

THE GORILLA
— FEEDING AND SOCIAL BEHAVIOR —

In the gorilla's forest habitat, it is easy for the gorilla to feed due to the year-round abundance of succulent plants and fresh shoots. All the animal has to do is reach out across the forest floor and grab a handful of greenery or find some ripe fruit.

The western lowland gorilla eats considerably more fruit than its eastern lowland cousin. It also tends to live in smaller groups containing about five individuals, since trees full of ripe fruit are too thinly scattered to support large groups of fruit-eating apes. Searching for the right fruit is a time-consuming activity, though in the persistent warmth of the gorilla's tropical home there is always a tree somewhere bearing ready-to-eat fruit. In the eastern part of their range, where the gorillas feed almost exclusively on the unlimited supply of green vegetation, groups may contain as many as 30 animals, though they more frequently consist of about 10.

The pattern of group membership is fairly constant. In an average group the silverback is accompanied by up to four females and five youngsters—immature females and "black-back" males of under 10 years.

The daily rituals

The gorillas' daily program begins at about seven o'clock in the morning, when they awaken and rise to feed for about two hours. They then rest for a while during the hottest part of the day, before feeding again until dusk falls at about six o'clock. Before bedding down for the night, the gorilla builds a nest of leaves slightly raised off the ground or on the ground itself—particularly in the case of larger males, which are much too big and heavy to attempt acrobatics in the trees.

During the day, when the gorillas are not feeding, they rest, groom, and play games (especially among the youngsters). Each group is headed by the silverbacked male. Relations among the individuals are generally friendly and when a subordinate gorilla finds itself in the presence of a superior, it merely allows the other animal to pass or stops whatever it is doing. Females with offspring may enjoy increased authority within the group while their offspring are young and vulnerable.

The relationships between female gorillas in a group are unstable, largely because they are unlikely to be related. Despite the lack of a fixed pair relationship among gorillas, sexual relationships tend to be carefully considered beforehand and are not conducted quickly as is the case in many other monkeys and apes.

Approaching a gorilla

Gorillas are gentle giants that will even accept humans as temporary group members, though this depends on humans behaving in the correct way. Although they are among the least aggressive animals on earth, gorillas that are surprised or frightened by people—especially old males defending family groups—may occasionally threaten and even attack humans. They can easily do serious damage to a person with their huge fists, strong arms and great weight. But this is very rare—

thousands of tourists have been within a few yards of wild gorillas without being threatened at all. In order to befriend a gorilla, humans should adopt non-threatening behavior such as quiet grunts and downcast eyes and be careful of their movements.

Male gorillas sometimes practice infanticide—killing a female's offspring on taking her into his group. This action helps to perpetuate the killer's genes rather than those of another male, since the female will soon be receptive to mate again after the death of her baby.

Obviously, a female will avoid infanticide as far as possible and she will not necessarily stay with (or mate with) the first male she meets after leaving her family group. She may transfer to another male if he is larger, stronger and more able to defend her against rivals and possible infanticide.

LEFT Two main periods of feeding occur during the mountain gorilla's day. The first takes place in the morning after the animal has awakened and the second between midday and sunset, after which the animal prepares its "nest" for the night.
ABOVE RIGHT AND RIGHT Adult gorillas often rest on low tree branches or relax on the ground between one meal and the next.
ABOVE Gorillas sometimes use large leaves as parasols to protect themselves from the strong rays of the equatorial sun.

been exploited in films and advertising. It should be remembered, however, that generally only the young chimpanzees are playful. As they mature, chimpanzees become stronger and more preoccupied, showing a greater interest in establishing hierarchies, feeding and reproducing.

Unfortunately, the chimpanzees' close relationship to humans may be their downfall. Because about 99 percent of their genetic material is identical to that of humans, large numbers of chimps are captured and collected in the wild and brought to Europe and America to be used in medical research. Coupled with habitat destruction, this threatens wild populations of chimpanzees in many areas.

There are two chimpanzee species, the common and the pygmy chimpanzees, and they are similar in many respects. The common chimpanzee reaches up to about 35 in. in length in the male and 33 in. in the female, and the sexes weigh up to about 187 lbs. and 154 lbs. respectively. The pygmy chimpanzee reaches up to approximately 31 in. in the male and 29 in. in the female. But it is in their weight that the main difference between the two species is apparent: the pygmy chimpanzee is a slighter animal than its close relative, the male weighing up to only 110 lbs. and the female 66 lbs.

ABOVE Watercourses have a marked effect on the distribution of gorillas, wide rivers forming permanent barriers to their movement. The animals will not enter the water and will cross rivers only if there are sufficent large, stable stones to prevent them getting wet. They seldom drink since they obtain enough liquid from the fruit and plant material they eat, and so they have no need to become used to water.

Varied foods

Chimpanzees are generally more agile than orangutans and gorillas. Their arms are much longer than their legs, and all four limbs are more slender than those of the gorilla. Their hands and feet are also noticeably longer.

The agility of chimpanzees is put to good use when it comes to reaching the tree-growing fruit of which they eat a great deal. They supplement this diet with other vegetable matter as well as obtaining protein from animals as varied as ants, termites, caterpillars and small or young mammals, including antelopes, pigs and monkeys.

The chimpanzees' thick, dark fur is shiny in healthy animals. It is usually black, but there is some variation in color, with brown tints occurring quite often. Older common chimps sometimes have a whitish beard. The white tail tuft seen in chimpanzees in films

and circuses is a feature of young common chimpanzees, and is present only during the first few years of life. In the pygmy chimp, the white tuft often persists into adulthood. The pygmy chimp's topknot often divides and sticks out to each side. In both species, older animals may become bald, and the coat on their backs may turn gray.

The face, the palms and soles and the genito-anal region of chimpanzees are hairless. They vary from shades of pink to brown, although the face is black in mature animals. In females, during the period of sexual receptivity, the skin around the external genital organs swells up and becomes deep pink in color.

Different habitats

Although they are more at home in the trees than gorillas, chimpanzees spend about two-thirds of their time on the ground, and occupy open as well as forested areas. The distribution of the chimps is not continuous. Different chimpanzee populations have become adapted to different environmental conditions. There is much habitat variation within their range, from the humid forests west of the River Niger to the more arid regions in the east, where chimpanzees can be found both on the plains and at higher altitudes.

Researchers have produced an enormous amount of information on chimpanzees in the wild and in captivity, and we now have a fairly accurate picture of their habits and social life. Many books have been written on the chimp's extraordinary learning ability in captivity and its behavior in the wild. Perhaps the best-known account of the chimpanzee's life is *In the Shadow of Man* by Jane Goodall.

The social organization of chimpanzees is more complex than that of gibbons, gorillas and orangutans, and involves a mixture of individualism and social behavior. Chimpanzees live in communities of

ABOVE RIGHT Like all social primates, baby chimpanzees require the contact of a group of adults and other youngsters in order to grow up normally. Young animals that are isolated and grow up on their own either die or become severely disturbed. Such isolation is sometimes the fate of laboratory animals that are taken from the wild.
RIGHT Caressing and grooming are two of the caring activities that the mother chimp provides for her young offspring. The infant is completely dependent upon her for the early part of its life, and is not weaned until it is about four years old.

between about 15 and 100 animals, and they occupy home ranges that vary from only a few square miles to over 38 square miles. Some of their range may overlap with the home ranges of other communities, but the groups usually avoid one another.

The community is broken up into subgroups or parties, each containing two to five animals. These parties may be all-male, all-female, all-young, or contain combinations of sex and age such as adult females and males, and adults and young. There is a fluid and ever-changing pattern of association between individuals, so that the parties do not always remain the same. Each chimpanzee tends to have its own "core area" where it sleeps and spends most of its time. Chimpanzees roam the community's whole home range but rarely travel alone. Females take their offspring with them and often join up with males, while the males are more sociable and often form partnerships and groups.

True family groups do not exist among chimpanzees, and females usually mate with more than one male. Females do not become pregnant on most occasions after mating, despite the fact that mating takes place only when they are receptive. Social bonds may be formed or strengthened by the act of mating, giving it an importance beyond reproductive needs.

ABOVE LEFT Although there is no strict hierarchy among chimpanzees, males establish a scale of importance based on physical strength and intelligence. In a group observed by the zoologist Jane Goodall, one male became the dominant animal because he made his charges more alarming by throwing tin cans.
ABOVE A chimpanzee removes the leaves from a stick so that it can be used as a tool, perhaps for getting termites out of a mound, or to add menace to a threat display.

Mating time

The female chimpanzee shows she is ready to mate by giving off certain smells and by the changing state of her genital area, which swells and turns more pink in color. During the time the female is in heat (or in "estrus"), she arouses great interest among the males. Females are in heat every four to six weeks for two to three weeks or more.

For the first week or so of being in heat, the female may mate with a number of males. They seek to attract her with fixed stares, violent branch shaking and calls, the exact pattern varying between populations. These signals may threaten her, suggesting that the males may attack her if she does not give in, and they can be enough to persuade the most reluctant of females to accept the males' advances. As a female approaches ovulation, the males become increasingly competitive

over her. The more powerful chimps chase away and threaten the young and low-ranking males that were allowed to mate with her early in her estrus. In this way, these dominant animals give themselves the best chance of siring the next generation.

Speedy mating

Mating takes only a few seconds. During the sexual act, young animals still under their mother's protection may stay beside the couple. They occasionally attempt to separate them, behaving aggressively toward the male, perhaps misinterpreting his actions as an attack on their mother. The males are extremely tolerant in these situations and take little notice of the young animals' attacks.

Male chimpanzees display great sexual vigor and may mate with one or more females up to 20 times in one day. They appear to take a casual attitude to mating, and during the sexual act the male may happily continue to eat. Several males may, moreover, take turns to mate with the same female.

In some chimpanzee populations, a female in heat forms a temporary association or consortship with one of the males, and the two leave the group for anything from a few days to several weeks in order to spend a "honeymoon" together. Interestingly, although most

ABOVE Although chimpanzees are mainly vegetarian, feeding chiefly on fruit, they also eat small amounts of animal food, including insects and small mammals, and even the young of larger mammals such as baboons. The search for food occupies most of the chimpanzees' waking hours—their mixed **diet requires them to forage more extensively than the vegetarian gorillas. PAGES 870-871 Between periods of feeding activity, groups of chimpanzees often rest in trees. Though chimps form large communities of up to 100 strong, they split up into small foraging groups during the day.**

matings are promiscuous, the female is more likely to become pregnant from mating during the period of her consortship. During pregnancy and for several years after birth, common chimpanzee females are not sexually receptive. Pygmy chimp females, however, continue mating during these times.

Long-lasting bonds

The gestation period lasts between about 200 and 260 days and births are single, twins being rare. The baby chimp, like a human baby, is helpless. A few days after birth it is able to cling to its mother's belly as she moves about, transferring to her back at about six months of age. At four years old the chimp is weaned and walking about independently. It leaves the mother

around the time of puberty, reached by about the age of seven or eight. Ties between mother and offspring seem to remain for many years and perhaps throughout life, and the animals always greet each other on meeting and groom one another.

Females do not normally give birth until they are at least 13 years old, while males are not fully adult until they are 15 years old. Females give birth, on average, every three years and can still breed at 30 years of age; many do so for longer—up to 45 years in some cases.

Competitive chimps

In many primates, particularly the monkeys, the males frequently compete for dominance in the group. Apart from the advantages this brings in feeding and grooming, it can also earn the dominant male the right to be the first to mate with the females of the group—ensuring that he will father a greater number of offspring than his fellow males.

The chimpanzees studied by Jane Goodall displayed a degree of competition and rivalry among the various males, and the hierarchies she observed were much more changeable and temporary than in other primates. Since males and females are sexually promiscuous all the time, it is impossible for one male to monopolize the females in the group. If most of the mature male chimps are free to mate, then the main reason for maintaining a strong and stable hierarchy—sexual dominance—is absent.

With this flexible set of relationships in the community, male chimpanzees have more opportunities to breed than any of the other social primates. Males tend to remain in the community in which they were born. As their turn will come to father offspring, there is not the same need that occurs in most primates to leave and start a new group.

To avoid the damaging effects of inbreeding, female chimps move out of their community when they come into heat soon after reaching puberty, and migrate to another chimp community nearby. Attracting some

ABOVE LEFT A young chimpanzee stays with its mother until it is about seven years of age. During this period, the young animal observes the behavior of its mother and other chimps, gradually learning all it needs to know in order to survive as an independent animal.
LEFT Chimpanzees are not entirely arboreal, but they are much more agile in the trees than gorillas and they can leap distances of up to 33 ft. from one branch to another.

male followers, they then roam their new community's home range, eventually establishing their own "core area." The males that accompany them in the first few months help to protect them from any aggression shown by well-established females.

Whose offspring

The male chimpanzees in each group are bound by a shared interest in defending the group's home range. Furthermore, as males apparently cannot recognize their own offspring within the group, all the community's youngsters benefit from the defense given by the adult males.

When chimpanzees have a dispute they usually reach a swift and bloodless conclusion by adopting an elaborate array of greetings, as well as gestures of submission and appeasement. Social rank is not marked by any particular external sign: dominant individuals need not be the biggest animals with the thickest coats or have the largest muscles. Instead, factors such as aggression and experience determine which of its fellows a chimpanzee can dominate.

Chimps on patrol

The dominant males are responsible for defense of the home range and protecting the group against enemies. The group leaders' efforts are rewarded by certain privileges, such as more frequent and intense grooming and first pick of the best fruit on a tree.

The males form patrol groups that travel to and around the perimeter of the community's home range—often waiting for hours to spot neighboring chimps. These patrol groups may contain a varying number of individuals, but the larger ones usually come off best in encounters with groups of chimpanzees from neighboring home ranges.

ABOVE Chimpanzees sometimes use overhanging trees in order to leap across streams. Like gorillas they do not swim, and rivers otherwise become an impossible barrier to cross.

BELOW Small chimps cling onto their mother's chest and belly, but when they are about seven months old they are carried on her back. They do not walk on their own until they are several years old.

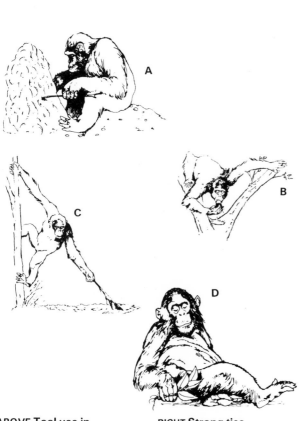

ABOVE Tool use in chimpanzees: digging for termites with a stick (A); using chewed leaves as a sponge for drinking rainwater (B); using a stick to capture red ants (C); cleaning the fur using a bunch of leaves (D).

RIGHT Strong ties sometimes appear to exist between brother and sister chimps. Studies of males in particular show that they can easily recognize their brothers and often maintain long-term friendships with one another.

Give-away calls

Patrol groups establish their own boundaries and work out the size of the patrol group ranked against them by calling and then listening to their neighbors' answering calls. The smaller group will tend to retreat.

When a patrol group spots an individual from another community, the patrolling chimps may chase and attack it, brutally beating and biting the animal with their large, sharp canine teeth. These attacks can be so vicious, and the chimp so badly mauled by its neighbors, that it will die from its injuries. Chimpanzee males often travel in groups, in which dominant males take submissive males along with them so that they can confirm their dominance from time to time through ritual attacks and gestures of display.

Separate diets

There are some dietary differences between the chimpanzees that inhabit dense forest and those that live in more open, arid areas. Forest chimpanzees live mainly on fruit and other plant matter, supplementing their diet with small invertebrates. Chimpanzees inhabiting the more open parts of their range often kill and eat larger animals. Wild boar piglets and monkeys, including young baboons, are chased, cornered, caught, killed (usually by picking them up by the hind legs and striking their heads against the ground) and then eaten.

Collective hunting involves a large degree of cooperation between individuals. It is a form of behavior commonly displayed by other mammals (for example,

wolves and lions) as well as primates, and it must have been of great importance in the early evolution of human communities.

Chimpanzees show great ability in handling tools, and females are considered to be more skilled than the males. They "fish" for both termites and ants with the aid of long sticks. To reach termites, the chimps insert sticks or strands of grass into the tunnels of termite mounds: these are aggressively grasped by the soldier termites, which lock their jaws around the stick. The chimpanzee waits until several termites are attached to the probe and then pulls it out of the hole. It then picks the termites off one by one and eats them. Female chimpanzees are usually responsible for these termite-catching activities.

Chimpanzees are able to recognize the tunnel entrances from which winged termites emerge, and they concentrate on these, digging with their fingers at the entrances before inserting their sticks.

A younger chimp often watches the termite-catching operations of its mother, and tries to imitate them. Its attempts might be unsuccessful at first, but the young chimp will eventually succeed.

Picking off soldiers

Chimpanzees use the same "fishing" technique to catch the soldier ants that tramp the forest paths in their long, unstoppable single files. Females set out with the deliberate aim of hunting these insects, preparing their sticks in advance. Once she has chosen a long, flexible wand, the chimpanzee strips it of leaves, cleans it, tests its suitability and then sets off in pursuit of her quarry.

It may take a while to find an army of soldier ants, but once the insect convoy has been found, the chimpanzee places the stick among the marching ants. Many will cling on to it with their powerful jaws, instinctively attacking this "intruder" into their column. They are picked off and eaten. Since soldier ants can deliver painful bites, the chimpanzee must keep her distance from the insects to avoid attack. For this reason the "fishing rod" is of considerable length.

It is unlikely that all this preparation and skilled technique is solely a result of instinct. The chimps' actions suggest that they are aware of what they are doing, deciding on their actions beforehand and taking the necessary precautions.

Tool-using talents

There are plenty of other examples of tool use among chimpanzees. In the Gombe Stream region of Tanzania, where Jane Goodall and other researchers have managed to establish friendly relations with the chimpanzees, the animals are regularly fed with bananas so that they can be observed at close quarters. But the fruit is placed in closed metal cases that must be opened, so that each individual can obtain its share. To get at the fruit, the chimpanzees resorted to using sticks as levers to raise the lids. In laboratories, chimps will use sticks to reach fruit hung beyond arm's length outside their cage.

Wild chimpanzees even use their own version of toilet paper. Chimp droppings are rather loose as a result of a diet consisting mainly of fruit. They therefore have to take great care if they are not going to dirty their fur, and they often clean their anal region very thoroughly. Many chimpanzees use wads of leaves like toilet paper to avoid dirtying their hands.

A leafy sponge

Forest-dwelling chimpanzees often drink rainwater that has collected in hollow trees. Instead of scooping up the water with their hands like gibbons and other apes, chimps have perfected a much more efficient technique. They make a kind of sponge by chewing up leaves and then dipping the absorbent mass in water. They can collect much more water in this way than they could hold in their hand, and only need to

squeeze the sponge into their mouths to get the liquid.

Chimpanzees often throw stones, twigs and pieces of wood during their threat displays. They show great throwing skill and do not hesitate to use sticks to hit potentially dangerous animals or to kill prey.

On one occasion, a chimpanzee was observed to throw stones at a female wild pig. The pig, hit by a stone thrown accurately from quite a few yards away, was sufficiently shocked and surprised to run off, leaving its young to be captured and eaten by the chimps.

Defensive instinct

Experiments carried out in the wild show how chimps defend themselves against leopards, their most feared predator. Using a life-sized stuffed leopard, the Dutch naturalist Adriaan Kortlandt observed that chimpanzees—particularly those inhabiting arid habitats where leopards occur—did not hesitate to attack the enemy and hit it with sticks. Although it was mainly the more powerful male chimpanzees that attacked the leopard, some females too, with their offspring on their shoulders, were observed to beat the fake predator savagely with sticks.

In one experiment, the chimpanzees attacked the stuffed leopard with such fury that one of the more aggressive and courageous males succeeded in knocking its head off. The chimpanzees immediately lost all interest in the big cat and some females even let their offspring approach closely enough to touch it. The chimpanzees were able to recognize that a headless animal does not represent a threat since there can be no doubt that it is dead.

Even though the chimps' use of weapons is unusual, advanced and relatively sophisticated, the recognition of a predator, and the degree of threat it represents, is common to a great range of animals, especially vertebrates such as birds.

Flo and Flint

When J. MacKinnon carried out his observations of chimpanzees in the Gombe Stream National Park in northwest Tanzania (alongside Lake Tanganyika) in 1966, he noted that the first chimp to discover the

RIGHT A chimpanzee probes rotting wood with a stick, effectively "fishing" for ants. When the stick is thrust among them many of the ants instinctively attack the intruding object and clamp their jaws on it. The chimp pulls the stick out, removes the ants and eats them.

technique of fishing for termites with slim sticks and grass stems was an elderly female that he named Flo. Her male offspring, Flint, watched her very closely, and occasionally picked up a stick discarded by Flo and tried a little fishing of his own. He proved a poor student, and it took him a long time to become as expert as his mother. However, a number of other adult females learned the technique from Flo, and passed it on to their own offspring.

Chimpanzee culture

It is easy to see how such a useful technique could spread throughout a chimpanzee colony, to be handed down through the generations. The first step, the actual discovery of the fishing technique, might have been a chance event—a chimpanzee idly poking a stick into a termite's tunnel, pulling it out and discovering termites on it. It could also have been made by a highly intelligent individual—a genius among chimpanzees. Such individuals are not common, and if they did not pass on what they knew or had discovered, techniques like termite fishing with sticks would never be known by the majority of chimpanzees. Any newfound technique might well be lost with the death of its discoverer.

Passing on skills and new ideas to other members of the group—known as "cultural transmission"—is therefore very important within a chimpanzee community. Each individual benefits from his or her own discoveries, and the discoveries of all the other members. Each generation discovers new ways of doing things, and adds them to the techniques learned from their parents—and so the cultural wealth of the species is built up. In chimpanzees it is a slow process, but among humans, as we know, innovations can spread very quickly.

Changing habits

In another observation, the researchers noted that the Gombe Stream chimpanzees abandoned well-established forms of behavior and adopted new ones. At one stage, for example, the chimpanzees took to building their night nests in the palm trees. On another occasion it became fashionable to hunt baboons instead of patas monkeys. These changes of behavior probably occurred in the same way that the termite probing came about: one individual started acting differently, and the others followed suit. If the

ABOVE The pouted lips of an adult chimpanzee are a gesture of greeting to other members of its group.
FAR RIGHT TOP As a young chimp grows, it learns the art of grooming, plucking out dirt and parasites from its mother's fur.

FAR RIGHT BOTTOM Different postures adopted by chimps when moving through the trees: climbing using all fours (A); swinging from a branch (B); grasping with three limbs (C); brachiating (D); jumping to the ground (E).

change in routine has significant advantages, the chimpanzees may adopt it permanently, or at least add it to their repertoire.

Skilled imitators

The speed with which these new behavioral variations spread through the colony—nesting in palm trees and hunting baboons—probably has something to do with the fact that they are easy to imitate, unlike tool use, which demands some dexterity. The researchers at Gombe Stream found that the chimps were highly skilled imitators. Indeed, the chimpanzees often mimicked the actions of their companions long before they understood the significance of the new behavior.

The animals imitated not only the actions of other chimpanzees, but also those of the researchers and their local helpers. MacKinnon describes one such occasion. One day he spent some time peering at a tree trunk, closely observing a jumping spider that was chasing a fly. A young female chimp named Fifi—the daughter of the termite-fishing Flo—had noticed MacKinnon's behavior from her vantage point on a nearby branch.

As soon as MacKinnon left the tree trunk where the jumping spider was finishing its meal, Fifi bounded

ABOVE The faces of chimpanzees are highly flexible. Special muscles supplied by a fine network of nerves enable them to produce a range of facial expressions, their complexity unmatched in all other primates except humans. When studying a group of chimps it is possible to recognize individual animals by their faces, just as it is with people. Recognition is aided by each individual's characteristic attitudes and way of moving around.

down to take his place, and began to observe the spider with equal intensity. But since she found little of interest in the sight of a spider eating a fly, she wandered away dissatisfied—no doubt wondering what the man had found so riveting. Had MacKinnon been engaged in some useful activity, she would have found out what he was doing, and would possibly have learned another skill.

A family trait

As with humans, intellectual ability among the chimpanzees of Gombe Stream seemed to be mainly inherited. The offspring of Flo, certainly one of the group's most intelligent members, were also clever, and Fifi sometimes showed signs of true inventive genius. She was intensely curious and would always closely inspect any object she came across. Many of the Gombe Stream researchers almost came to believe that every time Fifi handled an object, such as a branch of a slightly unusual shape, she was really wondering how she could use it.

Fifi's intelligence had a cunning edge to it, evident from her way of dealing with the cases of bananas put out by the researchers. She was well aware that if she opened a box in the presence of a stronger, higher-ranking male chimpanzee, she would undoubtedly have to give up her booty and be left empty-handed. But she found a way around the problem that showed considerable intelligence. After checking that no one was paying her close attention, she loitered by the metal case and gradually loosened the fastenings by unscrewing the nuts. She then waited until there was no one nearby—particularly male chimps—before giving the final twist, opening the box and making off with an armful of bananas.

A nest with a roof

Fifi was also, as far as the researchers knew, the first chimpanzee in the colony to make a nest with a roof. While preparing a nest in a high palm tree, she carried on folding leaves and adding branches until she had formed a great lopsided mound of plant matter. Rather than flattening it out, she decided to weave the stems into a kind of hood that projected over the nest. She obviously appreciated the advantage that the hood brought because she returned to the same nest on the following day, and made no further changes to it. In an area prone to sudden showers, she was better off than the other chimpanzees, whose conventional nests had no such protection against the weather.

The chimpanzees' rain dance

From the behavior of chimpanzees during rain showers, it appears that the apes do not like rain. Jane Goodall noticed that the Gombe Stream chimpanzees would often perform what she called a "rain dance." Before a shower, they made a series of apparently ritual gestures that seemed to be connected with fear, and that looked like an attempt to build up each other's confidence before a frightening event. Many human ritual dances are carried out in much the same spirit—although they have been described as dances to appease the forces of nature—and it is possible that they stem from the same root as those of the chimps.

New ideas are adopted and spread through the

ABOVE Like human children, young chimpanzees spend a great deal of time playing together, acting out behavior that they have copied from their elders. They become aware of sex roles at an early age; young males imitate the mating displays of adults, while young females show a strong interest in the care of baby chimps.

community with great speed, thanks to the chimp's ability to transmit information to the rest of the group. If chimpanzees had to inherit new skills and habits through the slow process of evolution, it would take hundreds of generations before they became established, and they could never be as flexibly employed as they are for having been learned. However, although learned behavior may be valuable in certain conditions, a chimpanzee will quickly abandon it if it is not appropriate to the situation at hand.

Learning the hard way

Learning can be a risky business, however. Much of it relies on trial and error. The errors often reinforce the learning process—providing the human equivalent of a sharp rap on the knuckles when things go wrong. But in certain circumstances, mistakes can prove disastrous. A chimp experimenting with different foods, for instance, might discover that a fruit is

ABOVE The near-human characteristics of chimpanzees have long attracted curious spectators, and in the past, captive animals were condemned to a life of close confinement in inadequate cages.

ABOVE RIGHT Today the trend in zoos is toward maintaining large breeding colonies of chimpanzees kept in more naturalistic enclosures that try to re-create elements of their true habitat.

poisonous only after eating it, or find out the hard way that a scorpion is dangerous. If the error proves fatal, then that knowledge will die with the victim, leaving others to make the same mistake.

In great apes like the chimpanzees—and even more so in humans—the replacement of instinctive reactions by learned behavior leaves young, ignorant individuals open to all kinds of danger. They will be vulnerable until they have learned how to cope with strange situations. This is one reason why the period of parental care is so extended; the young have to be taught how to survive, and protected while they learn.

Strict control

Most of what adult chimpanzees know is acquired when they are young, partly through instinct, but largely through learning. Young chimps show great

curiosity, initiative and a will to learn. But since too much curiosity can be dangerous, the adults exercise strict control over them in order to stop their explorations from getting out of hand.

A mother chimpanzee allows her offspring a certain amount of freedom, but she is always watchful. If the youngster does something that she is uncertain about, she will often put an end to it—sometimes quite violently. At Gombe Stream, for example, the chimpanzee Flo once pulled her son Flint away from a grasshopper with which he was playing. She even picked up the insect and flung it into the bushes. This was, on the face of it, curious behavior on her part. The grasshopper was obviously no threat to Flint. Even if the young chimpanzee had put it in his mouth, he would have spat it out on finding that it was inedible. But it is probable that Flo took a firm line on this occasion to impress on her offspring the dangers of playing with insects—the harmless grasshopper might have turned out to be a venomous scorpion.

A cautious mother

Flo proved cautious in her approach to unfamiliar plant food, and even prevented her offspring from eating papayas, which she was unsure about. Papayas are, in fact, perfectly edible, and in West Africa, forest

LEFT AND ABOVE The pink face of a young male chimpanzee from West Africa (left) contrasts strongly with the black face and ears of an adult chimp (above). The young animal's face will darken as he gets older. Both youngster and adult display the fringe of white beard that they keep throughout their lives. The hair on the young chimp's head is still fairly thick, but he will probably get progessively balder; the female (above) has already acquired an extensive bald patch.

chimpanzees eat them regularly. The West African chimpanzees, however, avoid several bushy plants that are commonly eaten by East African chimps. Such caution has often been mistaken for stupidity; nevertheless, where there is a possibility of poisoning, the chimpanzees would rather be safe than sorry.

Chimpanzees rarely suffer from boredom in the wild, and during the hottest part of the day they are happy to remain quietly in one place—resting, sleeping, grooming one another and letting the youngsters play. They show initiative even in the most unfavorable surroundings, and can usually find something to eat, a place to rest and some way of occupying their time. Chimpanzees are at their most imaginative when they are at play; any excuse and an object will be used to start a game. Young

chimpanzees love to play the kinds of games that are so familiar to human children: blind man's buff, wrestling, swinging, and jumping.

Sex roles at play

The sex of the chimpanzees determines what games they play. Young males show great interest in wrestling, imitating the mating displays of adults and stone throwing. Female chimps prefer to play with chimps smaller than themselves. They examine, touch, groom and clean them, and sometimes go so far as to steal them from their mothers. Just as with other animals, games are an important means of learning, but whatever their ultimate purpose and importance at the time, they are played out of sheer pleasure. This is important, for it is their pleasure that prompts them to carry on playing—and learning.

Mother chimpanzees frequently have to drag their offspring away from their playmates when it is time for them to leave.

Many chimpanzees have shown a keen interest in the basic forms of music, such as drumming. An ability to appreciate tempo and rhythm is undoubtedly useful in helping them to produce and understand sound signals, particularly those that are used in communication and in the defense of territories. But chimps often beat out rhythms on hollow tree trunks with evident satisfaction, and for no apparent reason. Again, it is easy to draw a parallel with the persistent beat of much primitive music.

Sand drawings

The chimpanzee's sight is extremely well developed. Like all primates it has the ability to see colors, and

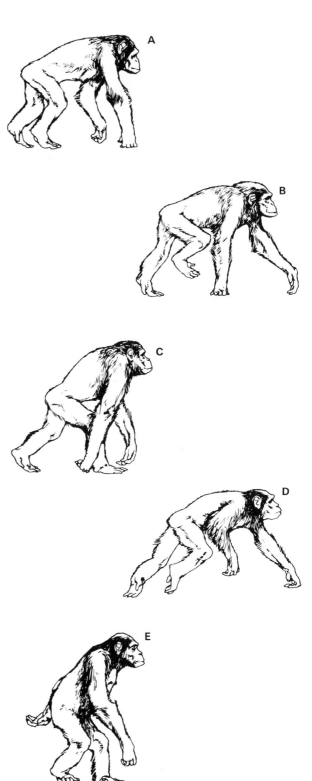

ABOVE **Foraging chimpanzees sometimes use established paths when moving across the forest floor from one feeding place to another.**
ABOVE RIGHT **The chimp is essentially a quadruped,** **but it can travel on just its hind legs for short distances. Here a chimp is shown walking slowly on all fours (A); walking quickly (B); running (C); sprinting (D); and walking upright (E).**

the position of its eyes gives it excellent binocular vision. This is useful when the animal is foraging for food, enabling it to distinguish between leaves and fruits more efficiently, but it also seems to give it a crude appreciation of visual art.

In the Gombe Stream National Park, several of the chimpanzees seemed to take pleasure from the shapes made in the sand by the wind, and even drew in the sand with their fingers. Chimpanzees that have been

ABOVE Young chimps show such an intense interest in their surroundings that mothers have to keep a sharp eye on their offspring. They have to make sure they do not tangle with potentially dangerous objects such as snakes or scorpions.

RIGHT Unusual for primates, male chimps often get on well, grooming one another and forming "gangs" that patrol territorial boundaries and pick fights with the neighbors. The parallel with human behavior is easy to make.

supplied with painting materials in captivity have often demonstrated an artistic skill that could be compared with that of very young children.

Communication

Although painting experiments with chimps in captivity are interesting, they are so divorced from the practical needs of chimpanzees in the wild that they tell us little about the chimps' real intelligence. It is in the area of communication that we find the most accurate reflection of the chimpanzee's perceptive powers and mental ability.

Chimpanzees, like many other monkeys and apes, produce a complex range of vocal signals, but in the chimps' case the sounds are often accompanied by gestures and attitudes that either reinforce the sound message or add an extra shade of meaning to it. Close

observation of chimps in the wild indicates that these signals are not used in a rigid way, with each sound always being accompanied by the same gesture. Instead the combination of sounds and gestures vary in detail each time. These subtle distinctions can change their meaning significantly, giving chimpanzees a much broader "vocabulary" than their normal vocal range would suggest.

The signals that chimpanzees use may only be expressions of emotion, without any communicative function, but from close study of wild and captive chimpanzees it is obvious that other individual chimps are well able to understand the slightest changes in the facial expressions of their companions. The Gombe Stream chimpanzees could even interpret the expressions of the researchers. The chimps used their eyes to communicate in the same way as

humans, and it is significant that researchers who have lived for some time with a group of chimpanzees usually come to a close understanding of each animal's character.

Sign language

Individual chimpanzees that have been reared together with human children often show striking "human" characteristics. Several individuals have been taught to communicate using sign language devised for the use of the deaf and dumb, learning many words and even forming sentences.

Even the more ritualized forms of chimpanzee behavior may be used with great subtlety. The act of submission made by a young animal to an adult is usually prompted by fear and a wish to ward off aggression. But a cunning chimpanzee may use it for a completely different purpose—to divert the attention of the adult, and enable the "submissive" animal to get away with some forbidden activity. When a young chimpanzee wants to steal a tasty morsel from an adult, it may lull the adult into a false sense of security by adopting an attitude of submission, before making off with the food when the rightful owner has relaxed its vigilance and become preoccupied.

A key to origins

Chimpanzees have always attracted interest, partly because they are fascinating to observe but also because they may help us understand the origins and biological basis of human behavior. There are many features of the chimpanzee way of life that recall our own. Like us, they live in a cooperative social system that still allows room for individual enterprise.

ABOVE With its protruding snout, prominent brow ridges and sloping forehead, the chimp's skull is clearly different from that of a modern human, but the most significant contrast between the two is the way the head is supported. In the ape, the spine is attached to the back of the skull, enabling the animal to look around when walking on all fours. Even in the most primitive humans, the skull is balanced on top of the spine, indicating that they, like us, walked upright.

Chimpanzees rely heavily on learning, as opposed to instinct. They make and use simple tools and weapons. In some areas they hunt and kill small or young mammals, and males will even indulge in a form of gang warfare.

There is no question of chimpanzees being our ancestors. They have developed along separate evolutionary lines for several million years, and probably bear only a passing resemblance to the common ancestors of apes and humans. Despite this, their behavior may give us some idea of how the early hominids (early ancestors of man) went about their daily business.

The pygmy chimpanzee

There are three races of common chimpanzees, varying in coloration but otherwise very similar. The behavior and degree of intelligence of wild chimpanzees seem to vary from one population to another as a result of local environmental conditions rather than race. However, there is one chimpanzee that is quite different in its appearance and behavior, and is considered to be an entirely separate species: the pygmy chimpanzee, or bonobo.

Despite its name, the pygmy chimpanzee is not noticeably smaller than its relative, the common chimpanzee. But although it stands almost as tall, it has a much lighter build. For years it was considered to be an undersized race of the common species, and its many individual features were not recognized until 1929 when museum specimens aroused the interest of an anatomist. He noted the slender body and pink lips that distinguish it from the much more widespread common chimpanzee.

Today pygmy chimpanzees are restricted to an area of tropical forest south of the Zaire River in Central Africa. They are isolated from other chimpanzees by the width of the river. In areas where the two species could mingle they seem to keep to themselves, with their own mating habits and way of life. There are no records of the two species interbreeding.

Pygmy chimp's menu

The forest favored by the pygmy chimpanzee is humid but not swampy, with plenty of secondary growth beneath the leaf canopy. The pygmy chimp gets much of its food from this lower level of the forest, including young shoots and leaves, and in this respect it resembles the ground-dwelling, leaf-eating gorilla. It also eats insects, some meat (although less than the common chimpanzee) and underground fungi, which it digs up. But the rest of its diet consists of fruit that it gathers from high up in the tall trees in the morning and late afternoon. (Pygmy chimps often descend from the trees at noon when the heat is greatest to forage on the ground for fallen fruit.)

The pygmy chimpanzee is much better adapted to treetop foraging than its larger cousin. Its lighter weight and more graceful build give it an agility in the treetops that a common chimpanzee lacks. It seems to have a sharper sense than common chimps of how much weight the branches can carry. Common chimpanzees frequently fall after trusting themselves to dead or damaged branches. The pygmy chimpanzee, in contrast, swings itself through the foliage with a casual confidence that is quite unlike the rather awkward, deliberate movements of the larger ape.

Safety in trees

The animal's preference for a more tree-dwelling life becomes apparent when it is alarmed. Whereas common chimpanzees often come down to the ground if they are frightened, pygmy chimpanzees do the opposite, climbing up into the biggest, tallest trees and hiding amid the foliage. They generally make their beds in trees. But despite this, the local people regard them as primarily ground-dwelling animals. There is little justification for regarding the species as an African equivalent of the gibbon, as some writers do. When the pygmy chimpanzee travels over the ground, it walks on its knuckles like the common chimpanzee and the gorilla, and may cover some distance this way. Its overland excursions, though, cannot compare with the long-distance hikes sometimes undertaken by common chimpanzees.

Social life

Pygmy chimpanzees seem to be more sociable than the larger species. They often gather together into large groups of up to 120 animals. More usually, they live in subgroups of 15 to 30, with a roughly even balance of males and females. These subgroups appear to be more stable than similar subgroups formed by common chimpanzees, and the same animals may travel together for a year or more.

Although quieter than common chimpanzees, pygmy chimpanzees can still make their presence known if they feel inclined. They rarely shriek and chatter, but do scream in fright or fear and they produce a curious, high-pitched, metallic alarm call. In general, pygmy chimpanzees do not seem to be as aggressive as common chimpanzees, although fights are still common: most adult males bear the scars of past skirmishes on their lips and ears.

Of uncertain origin

The precise origins of the pygmy chimpanzee are uncertain. Some zoologists believe that it probably evolved earlier than the common chimpanzee. Others consider it to be a relatively recent offshoot of the common chimpanzee stock. One interesting argument that has been advanced to support this theory involves a phenomenon known as "neotony." Neotony means

ABOVE **More lightly built than its cousin, but of a similar size, the pygmy chimpanzee is quite at home in the forest canopy, swinging from branch to branch with ease in search of the fruit that forms the greater part of its diet. Around midday** it descends to the cooler ground level and forages for fallen fruit, returning to the trees when it is time to sleep. Pygmy chimpanzees are becoming increasingly rare in the wild, and there are very few presently held in captivity.

889

the retention of infantile characteristics by a sexually mature adult.

In the case of the pygmy chimpanzee, a closer look at its body structure reveals that it has the proportions of a young common chimpanzee. It also shares other features such as a comparatively large head and, most noticeably, a tuft of white fur in the tail area that young chimps develop as a peace signal to older animals. Another juvenile feature is a smaller, more slender body. All this supports the idea that pygmy chimpanzees are a variant of the common chimpanzee stock in which overall body development is slowed down and sexual maturity accelerated.

The theory of neotony is an attractive one for many naturalists. If it is true, then it means that they pygmy chimpanzee evolved from the common chimpanzee so as to benefit from the abundant fruit that grows high in the forest canopy—most of which is out of reach of its heavier, clumsier relative.

It is not clear what natural enemies pygmy chimps have to face. They may suffer from attacks by leopards and, when in the treetops, by monkey-eating eagles that swoop down to catch the young.

Face to face

An interesting feature of the pygmy chimps is their mating behavior. The male does not display in front of the female. Instead, it is the female that usually encourages the male to mate. He clasps the female with one hand around her neck, and the other around her back, and they mate face to face in a reclining or crouching position.

Despite these apparently favorable adaptations, the pygmy chimpanzee does not seem to have fared very well. It is possible that, having become something of a specialist in its own habitat, it has sacrificed some of the adaptability that enables the common chimpanzee to thrive in a wide variety of environments. One reason for its rarity is that its range has become fragmented due to the destruction of its habitat.

UNDER THREAT

THE GREAT APES

All the great apes face threats in the wild, and some local populations have undergone severe declines in recent decades. The four species are all included in the most urgent category of CITES—the Convention on International Trade in Endangered Species—which seeks to regulate the export and import of endangered wildlife.

Orangutans have already become extinct in many of their former haunts. In the past the greatest threat to these apes came from capture of the animals, particularly the young, for use as pets or zoo exhibits. Not only did many of the infants die during transport, but in order to collect them from the wild, hunters usually had to shoot the mothers first. Nowadays the chief problem orangutans face is the clearance of their rain-forest habitat for logging and for agriculture. In Sumatra, land clearance has reduced their range by one-third since the 1930s.

Habitat loss, hunting, and the collection of live animals have combined to cut the numbers and distribution of all three races of the gorilla. Throughout its range the animal continues to suffer from forest clearance. In many places it is shot as a crop pest and for its meat; in others, there is even a souvenir trade in gorilla skulls. In the early 1980s the populations of the western and eastern lowland gorillas were estimated at about 14,000 and 5000 respectively, while in 1986 the number of mountain gorillas stood at about 300. The critically low population of the mountain gorilla has at least prompted measures to provide the animal with effective protection. For the present their numbers seem to be on the increase.

For chimpanzees the main threat, once again, is habitat destruction. Though they remain the most numerous of the great apes, they have suffered huge declines in some regions. In the 1940s the West African population stood as high as two million—40 years later it had collapsed to about 17,000. Hunting and collection have also taken their toll, and one of the main concerns of conservationists now is the continuing trade in chimps for use in medical research. To trap a young chimp, local hunters may first shoot or poison a whole group of adults—as many as 10 animals may die for each one that ends up in a research laboratory.

ON TWO LEGS

Over the last 30 million years, crouching forest primates left the trees and began to develop into modern humans—upright, dextrous and creative, but with the power to destroy

Two hundred years ago the idea of including human beings in an encyclopedia of animal life would have been unthinkable. In no way did people consider themselves animals. However, this view received a severe jolt in 1859 when Charles Darwin published the book *On the Origin of Species*—the product of more than 20 years of painstaking research. At the same time and quite independently, the naturalist Alfred Russel Wallace was engaged in similar study. The work of the two men proved beyond reasonable doubt that living things change their nature through time.

Individuals that are well equipped to survive and reproduce prosper and produce more young than their less well-equipped neighbors. In doing so, they pass on their genetic characteristics to the next generation, including those favorable genes that aided their survival. In the course of many, many generations the favorable characteristics are preserved and the number of individuals that possess them gradually multiplies. Meanwhile, other less favorable characteristics may be lost from the population altogether. In time, these gradual changes may result in the evolution of a new species. The process of change is known as natural selection.

Darwin chose to illustrate his theory by comparing modern and extinct forms of shellfish, particularly barnacles. His evidence consisted of living forms that can be found today on any rocky beach, along with their fossilized ancestors preserved within rocks. The implication of his work was plain: if you could find enough fossils, you could trace the ancestry of any modern creature back to its primitive beginnings—and that included humans.

LEFT When they first came to world attention in 1971, the Tasaday people of Mindanao island in the Philippines lived in ways similar to our Neolithic ancestors. The small group of 25 men, women and children wore loincloths, lived in caves in the rain forest, hunted animals and gathered wild fruit, yams, small fish, crabs and grubs. Unfortunately, they may have been a hoax. Reports have suggested that they belonged to a nearby and more culturally advanced tribe that had taken to living in caves under government pressure. PAGE 891 The upright stance of humans frees our hands to manufacture and manipulate tools with far greater skill than any other primate.

Incomplete evidence

Even today the precise ancestry of human beings is still in doubt, since the patchy nature of the fossil evidence means that there are vast gaps in our knowledge. Furthermore, though there have been several types of human-like animals walking the Earth at various times (just as today there are different species of monkeys), only our own species survives. We cannot, therefore, draw conclusions about our ancestry from comparisons of different living species, as zoologists frequently do with other animals. All the evidence has to be dug up; a few fragments here, a few there. The fossil fragments rarely fit together, and attempts to reconstruct remains can be misleading.

"Piltdown Man"

A notorious example was that of "Piltdown Man," reconstructed from an incomplete skull and jawbone found in an English gravel pit in 1912. All the fragments appeared to be of the same age, but while the skull—or what was left of it—was obviously human, the jaw appeared similar to that of an ape. Surely here was the "missing link" between apes and man—an intermediate stage in evolution that had retained the ape-like jaw but developed a large brain. The idea was attractive to those scientists who considered that intelligence was the most important of human attributes. Unfortunately it did not correspond with other evidence suggesting that, as humans evolved, their large brains developed after their human-like jaws. In 1953, on closer scrutiny, the Piltdown remains turned out to be exactly what they looked like—a human skull and the jaw of an ape—an orangutan to be precise. They had been planted in the gravel pit as part of an elaborate hoax.

The point was not lost on the general public. *On the Origin of Species* was an instant sensation, and the first edition sold out on the first day of publication. It became the focus of intense controversy, and the ensuing debate was fueled by Darwin's friend Thomas Huxley. It was Huxley who made the pronouncement that man and the apes were distant relatives, and that man had evolved from a creature very like a modern ape or monkey. This was heresy, and undermined the whole concept of creation (widely believed at the time, and laid down in the Old Testament of the Bible) that man was created by God within a few days of the creation of the world. Many refused to believe the new theory, and indeed it was hard to prove—unlike fossil shellfish, the remains of primitive man are very rare, and their relationship to each other is extremely difficult to ascertain.

LEFT A human's large, complex brain is fully developed at birth, with the result that a baby is born with a very big head for the size of its body. The large head makes birth a much more protracted and painful process than it is for most mammals. It also means that the baby has to be suckled for a long time to ensure that the development of its body catches up with its brain. Humans remain dependent on their parents for a longer period than any other animal.

The missing link

No one knows who perpetrated the hoax, or why, but one reason for its initial success was the popular belief in the "missing link." If man was descended from the apes, then surely there must have been a halfway stage, half ape and half human—an ape-man, in fact. The concept was so deeply rooted that when the first skull of a truly primitive human being was found in Java in 1893—and this one was authentic, with a human-type jaw and small brain—its discoverer Eugene Dubois christened it with the scientific name *Pithecanthropus erectus*. *Pithecus* means ape, *anthropus* means human, and *erectus* means "standing upright," so the whole name means "upright ape-man."

As we shall see later, the name was seriously misleading and was subsequently changed. Dubois' error resulted from a misunderstanding of human evolution. We are not descended from the apes; the chimpanzee, gorilla and orangutan are not our ancestors. Primitive humans were something else entirely. At the time they first appeared, the apes as we know them were only beginning to evolve.

Apes and humans are both descended from a creature that appeared over 30 million years ago, and they have developed along separate lines ever since. The original creature was a lemur-like primate called *Aegyptopithecus*, meaning "Egyptian ape." Small, agile, with a long snout and probably a long tail, it seems to have lived in the trees and fed on leaves and fruit in the formerly lush forests of North Africa. Its way of life was probably quite similar to that of the modern pygmy chimpanzee.

In due course, the animal gave rise to another group of primates called, collectively, *Dryopithecus*, whose fossilized remains have been found in Africa and Mediterranean Europe. These animals first appeared about 20 million years ago, and their remains recur again and again in the fossil record until about nine million years ago. They had many recognizably ape-like characteristics, and they are generally considered to be the ancestors of all the great and lesser apes. The belief cannot be proved, however, since there is a 9-million-year gap in the evidence following the disappearance of *Dryopithecus*. Quite simply, there are no fossil remains of the primitive apes that lived during those 9 million years, probably because the soils in their forest habitat were too acidic to preserve their bones.

The makings of a human

Fortunately, the creatures that evolved into modern humans (and their extinct relatives) often lived in places where the soils were not as corrosive, and more of their remains have survived. Even so, there are still large gaps in the fossil record. On the early side of one such gap is a creature called *Ramapithecus,* dating from some 13 million years ago. In many ways it appears to have been similar to *Dryopithecus,* but there was a significant difference between them. Instead of the long canine teeth and small molars typical of an ape, it had small canines and large molars, just as we do.

Ramapithecus was just one of a group of similar pre-human primates that lived in and around tropical Africa at a time when a general drying of the climate was encouraging the spread of open woodlands and grasslands. Such country does not suit the fruit-eating apes that prefer to stay within the forests, but it does favor animals that can live on the tough roots and seeds that are found in open country. Since *Ramapithecus* had large, flat grinding teeth and no protruding canines to impede chewing (to chew effectively you need to be able to move your jaw sideways, and interlocking canines would prevent such movement), it was well equipped to exploit the roots and seeds. In short, *Ramapithecus* and its cousins flourished in the increasingly open terrain.

Apart from its teeth, *Ramapithecus* had few obviously human traits. It was small—little more than 3 ft. high when standing up—and it seems to have spent a lot of its time on all fours. It could probably climb well, if only to escape from predators, and it may have slept in the trees like a modern chimpanzee. However, it may also have used primitive tools and weapons such as sticks and stones, and it must have walked upright at least some of the time, so that it could free its arms to use its hands. It was not a true human-like creature—a hominid—but it had the makings of one.

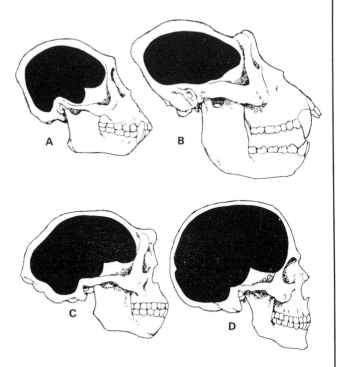

ABOVE A comparison of the skulls of a macaque (A), gorilla (B), *Homo erectus* (C) and *Homo sapiens* (D) shows how brain size increases through the monkeys, great apes, primitive humans and modern man. But absolute brain size is not always an accurate measure of intelligence—potential intelligence is best gauged by the size and surface area of the brain in relation to body weight.

Unfortunately, the large gap in the fossil evidence that occurs just after *Ramapithecus* means that we do not know how it developed later. It may or may not have given rise to the true hominids. Until someone finds the corresponding fossil, we cannot be sure. Meanwhile the period between 12 and 4 million years ago is a blank.

A hominid called Lucy

The fossil that marks the end of that vast gap in our understanding was discovered in 1974 in Ethiopia. Christened "Lucy" by her finders, she was a female hominid of a primitive type—not yet a human but much closer to one than *Ramapithecus*. She was just over 3 ft. tall, with a small brain and a chimp-like face, but her teeth were like those of a human, and she walked upright. The fossils prove that she walked erect because they include half of her pelvis—the bone is

THE PRIMATES

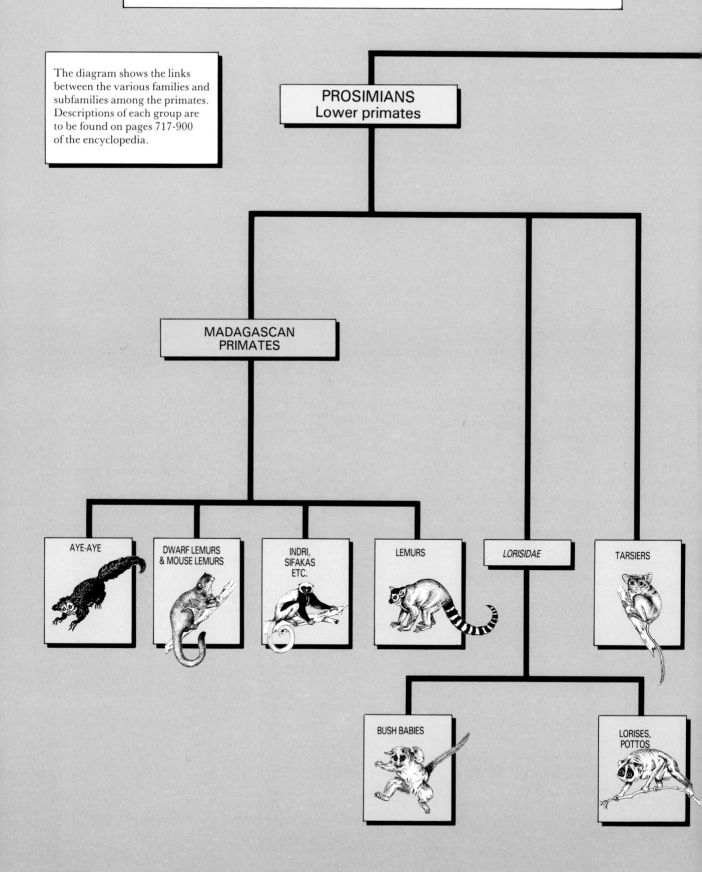

The diagram shows the links between the various families and subfamilies among the primates. Descriptions of each group are to be found on pages 717-900 of the encyclopedia.

PROSIMIANS
Lower primates

MADAGASCAN PRIMATES

AYE-AYE

DWARF LEMURS & MOUSE LEMURS

INDRI, SIFAKAS ETC.

LEMURS

LORISIDAE

TARSIERS

BUSH BABIES

LORISES, POTTOS

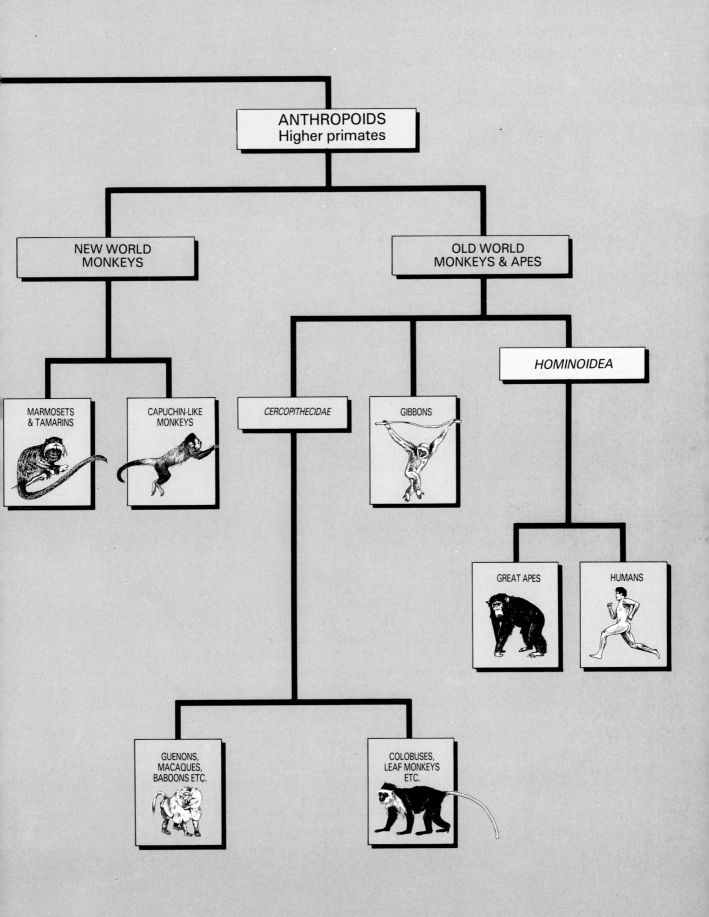

like that of a biped and quite unlike an ape's pelvis. And if further proof were needed, her excavators have even found some fossilized footprints.

After Lucy, the hominid line seems to have split into two. One line, known as *Australopithecus*, evolved into big-boned individuals that became increasingly well adapted to chewing tough plant food. As far as we know they did not make tools—although they probably used sticks and stones—and their brain capacity was limited. The line appears to have culminated in a strong-jawed type called *Australopithecus robustus*, also known as *Zinjanthropus* or Nutcracker Man—the latter giving a good idea of its chewing abilities.

The second line gave rise to another group of hominids . They were finer-boned, with smaller teeth and larger brains, and the remains of the earliest, dating from 1.75 million years ago, were found alongside primitive stone tools. The ability to manufacture tools is commonly reckoned to be a human trait, so these hominids were classed as true humans and given the generic name *Homo*. Their finders, Mary and Louis Leakey, called them *Homo habilis*—Handy Man—in recognition of their tool-making ability. Their remains were discovered in Tanzania's Olduvai Gorge in 1960. They stood about 5 ft. tall, and had a brain capacity of about 50 cubic inches—more than half the modern human average of 85 cubic inches.

Upright Man

The remains of all these hominids have been found in Africa, a continent that has been described as "the cradle of mankind." The species that apparently came after Handy Man, however, seems to have been a traveler, for its remains have turned up in Africa, Asia and Europe. It was the bones of this species that Eugene Dubois discovered in Java and named *Pithecanthropus erectus.* Unquestionably a human, it has since been renamed *Homo erectus,* Upright Man. It was rather taller than *H. habilis,* and its brain had a volume of some 40-80 cubic inches.

BELOW Man's adoption of an upright gait has involved a series of changes to the skeleton. A monkey (A) has slanting shoulder blades and long pelvic bones on which to anchor the muscles required for a quadrupedal gait (the shoulder blades and pelvic bones are shaded black). A gorilla (B) is also a quadruped, and retains the elongated pelvis, but because its long arms are adapted for swinging from branches, its shoulder blades have moved to the back of its ribcage. The shoulder blades of a human (C) are similar, but the pelvis has become shortened and flattened to support the muscles needed for an upright gait.

FAR LEFT By the beginning of the 21st century, the earth will be home to over six thousand million people inhabiting all but its most harsh environments. Roughly half that population will be crowded into towns and cities.

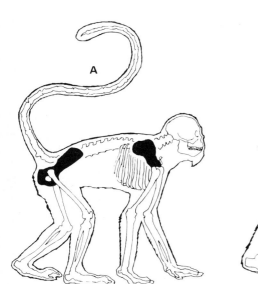
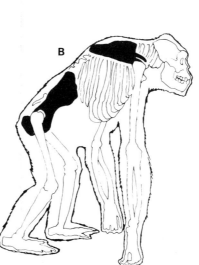
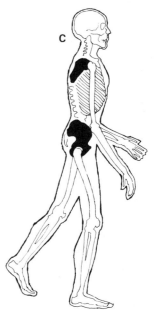

ABOVE Designed for bipedal walking, our long legs make it difficult for us to get about on all fours. Before a baby learns to walk, it has to crawl awkwardly on its hands and knees.
BELOW The macaque (A) has all four limbs the same length, and walks on its palms and soles. If a human child tries to do the same (B) it cannot easily see where it is going. The arms of a chimp (C) and a young gorilla (D) are longer than their legs, raising the position of their heads and improving their view. They can bring their heads even higher by standing on their knuckles.

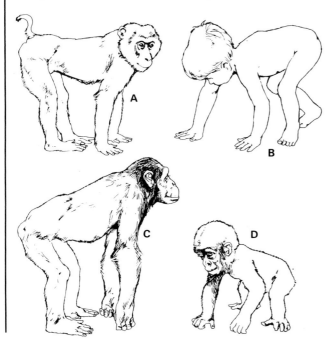

Our own species, *Homo sapiens*, emerged about half a million years ago. It is unclear whether we are the direct descendants of *H. erectus*, but at some point stocky, tough humans appeared that could cope with the rigors of the European ice ages. They were classified as *H. sapiens neanderthalensis*, and named Neanderthal Man after the place where their remains were found (the Neander Valley in Germany). Eventually they were ousted by a more refined type of human known as Cro-Magnon Man (*H. s. sapiens*), although it is quite possible that the two races interbred. Cro-Magnons were, to all intents and purposes, modern humans. They could hunt, make tools and utensils, paint pictures and develop complex religious theories. From that point it was a short step to herding, farming and the beginnings of the civilization that exists today. Highly adaptable and increasingly able to exploit the world's resources, human beings gradually became the most numerous and widespread of all the primates.